An Engineer's Space Race Stories and More

A collection of memories by Robert (Bob) Allen Munroe about his work life at 3 large US corporations; Raytheon, IBM, and Motorola. Including the B-58, Orbiting Astronomical Observatory, Gemini program, Saturn V guidance, Personal Computers, and the technologies involved.

Copyright © 2021 by Robert (Bob) Allen Munroe
All rights reserved.
ISBN: 978-0-578-87332-9

Author Biography

Born in Biddeford, ME in April 1936 and growing up in Watertown, MA, Nashua, and Hudson, NH I always have considered myself a New Englander despite living in NY, CA, AL, CO, and finally in TX.

I attended Lowell Technological Institute (merged into what is now UMass-Lowell) on a scholarship and graduated in 1958 with a BS in Textile Engineering which is basically mechanical engineering. With the benefit of a Raytheon scholarship I studied Engineering Physics at Harvard in 1959 but did not obtain an M.S.

I worked at Sanders Associates in Nashua, NH, Raytheon in Maynard, MA and in 1961 joined the Federal Systems Division (FSD) of IBM in Owego, NY and retired from IBM in 1991. I started work for the Motorola Semiconductor Division in Austin, TX after IBM and retired from Motorola in 2001.

I was fortunate to be awarded 2 Division and 2 IBM Corporate level awards and reached patent level awards at both IBM and Motorola. At IBM I was awarded management awards a total of three times at 2 different plants and 2 different divisions while in the role of an engineering manager.

Acknowledgements

Probably the most important man in my life was my uncle, Robert (Bob) Curtis Smith and I think I was named for him. After the divorce of my parents he and his wife Martha helped me in so many ways and I am forever thankful for him.

Another man important in my life was my stepfather (for over 60 years), John Franklin Blaney. He was a mechanic and never graduated from high school but could read a hydraulic diagram like text.

My high school chemistry teacher Marco Scheer PhD encouraged me to study and was a great mentor during my high school years.

My maternal grandparents Samuel E. Smith and Ruth Estelle Smith took care of me for 6 formative years and helped form me in so many positive ways. My grandfather's partner in the plumbing and heating business, Artemus Lovejoy a WWI veteran took me fishing and hunting at his cabin in northern N.H..

In my work life Hemenway Reginald Bullock who at one time was a tenured professor of metallurgy at M.I.T. (never had a degree). He was a department manager at Raytheon who treated us young people like family and introduced us to new technologies and several professors at M.I.T..

Fellow engineers like Bruno Pagnani, Bob Christiansen, Bill Singleton, Gary Fillmore, Tom Young, Ed Massey, and Charlie Wolfe supported me not only in my work but helped me grow on the job.

This story would not have been written without the encouragement of my wife Jane Kent Hedges and I am forever thankful to her.

This book would never have been published without the encouragement, support, and editing by Dr. Dede Casad and Maryam Mathis.

Foreword

This series of life stories is admittedly prone to faults and missing names because it is a record of my personal memories and memories are less than perfect. Any missing names where credit should be given or errors in facts are entirely my fault and I apologize in advance for them.

What is important I believe is to convey the overall view of life or work event so that the reader can get an idea of what goes on behind the scenes in work in large corporations. That is why I think of it as being an ant in an ant colony. E. O. Wilson calls organization of insects that act in a concerted way to accomplish a goal, a super organism. Each insect has a role to play but probably does not know what the overall goal is or even what it may accomplish I often thought of men and women in large corporations in this way. The lowest person or highest person rarely, if ever, knows what is going on in total or at best knows what their role is or the impact of their role in the immediate work environment. I was fortunate in several cases in IBM and Motorola to know the immediate impact of my contribution. Some of the experiences were not known to the larger population, and in a few cases known to very few for reasons that will be evident.

Some of the people I recall are as follows;
Bruno Pagnani who I met at IBM-FSD in Owego, N.Y. and have been in contact ever since. Several times we worked at the same plant. He was a fluid mechanics expert who obtained his PhD in mechanical engineering while at IBM. We met socially and our families knew each other. Bruno is retired in he Raleigh, N.C. area.

Ray Hagstrom a non-degreed court expert in metallurgy with extensive knowledge in casting, forging, welding, brazing, and soldering. I met Ray at Raytheon in1959 and he was a friend. My first wife Dorothy and I met socially with him and his wife Lorraine. He worked at IBM-FSD in Owego and is now deceased.

Jim Price was an electronic packaging design manager I supported and later worked for after I met him in IBM-FSD Owego. A great mentor of young engineers and he assembled a good team. He and his wife entertained some of us younger men and their families. I kept in touch with them after they left IBM-FSD in Thousand Oaks, CA. until they both died.

Bob Christiansen I met at IBM-FSD Owego and was a great organic materials expert and a good trouble shooter and problem solver in manufacturing. He moved to IBM-OPD in Lexington, KY and stayed on at that site after IBM sold it to Lexmark. He also did consulting for automotive suppliers in that area. Bob, a formidable race car driver in SCCA, raced a Chevrolet Camaro against national competition. Another family friend through the years died in 2019.

Bob Madeya I met at IBM-FSD Owego where he arrived after working at Boeing. He was an organic materials application expert and especially good in structural adhesives. Bob is retired and lives in New Mexico.

Don Fisher is an organic chemist and worked in the analytical area of the materials laboratory at IBM-FSD Owego.

Bob Gridley was a manager in the materials laboratory.

Roger Wild was the man that started as a metallurgical technician at IBM-FSD Owego and became a world renowned solder expert concerning creep and fatigue of solder joints in electronics. He along with Frank Ripp and Ray Hagstrom, were a formidable trio in electronic package solder applications. Roger probably stuck with it the most and had a consulting business after retiring from IBM-FSD Owego. He is deceased now.

There was so much talent at IBM-FSD Owego at that time in the so called materials lab. I can recall technicians like Doug Capwell, Gordon Hitt and Don Groover. There were others in skills like analytical chemistry and x-ray measurements, but unfortunately I cannot recall their names.

After a short stint (6 months) in Thousand Oaks, CA, where IBM never intended to stay in my opinion, I transferred to IBM-FSD in

Huntsville, AL. I reported to Ed Massey there and his boss was Ken Harris an absolutely great guy who treated his people well and no one worked harder than he did.

After Huntsville I transferred to IBM-OPD in Boulder, CO. I was in a small team with Gary Fillmore and we were managed by Tom Young. Gary had a PhD in Information Theory and Tom had an M.S. in optics so both were well versed in mathematics. Both had transferred from IBM-OPD in Lexington after starting at IBM in Endicott, N.Y.. I learned more from both of them than they know and we kept in touch after I left Boulder. Gary is retired and lives in CA and Tom is deceased.

I left Boulder to go to work for IBM-OPD in Austin, TX and I reported to Ed Massey. Ed was very patient with me and he led a group doing electrical design and my job was to form a special circuits group making hybrid electronic circuits. Charlie Powers was our manager and he had sold the corporation on building personal computers and similar assemblies using 100 % surface mount technology when personal computers (PCs) were assembled using holes in the printed circuit boards to receive components with leads that were placed through the holes and soldered. Unfortunately, Charlie's dream was a little early and component manufacturers were not always up to the task to make reliable components to mount on top of the boards. Today surface mount technology is used in most consumer electronics.

Circuit designers I recall in Austin were Gus Schrottke, Chip Conklin, and Ken Rhyner was a computer aided designer (CAD) specializing in printed circuit boards (PCBs) and hybrid circuit layout. Ron Crawford was also a CAD designer like Ken and retired in FL.

Tom Dillon was a key engineer reporting to me as we built up the hybrid circuit laboratory. Danny Massey, Ed Massey's son, was a technician and today is a high level design manager in IBM.

Table of Contents

Author Biography		iii
Acknowledgements		iv
Foreword		v
Chapter 1	Early Work History	1
Chapter 2	OAO	6
Chapter 3	Gemini	11
Chapter 4	MMRBM	25
Chapter 5	Saturn V	28
Chapter 6	We Didn't Do That	50
Chapter 7	4Pi Computers	57
Chapter 8	Hybrid Circuits	62
Chapter 9	Ink Jet Laboratory	77
Chapter 10	Hybrid Circuits & Worldwide Manufacturing	85
Chapter 11	My Time With Motorola	95
References		103

Chapter 1
Early Work History

After high school or perhaps as early as my last year of high school I went to work at Sanders Associates. This was a defense oriented high technology firm that was in an old mill building on Canal Street in Nashua, N.H.. When the assets of all the mills were purchased by Roy Little of Textron the empty buildings were purchased by the city I think or were purchased at a very low price by a city coordinated development organization. Entrepreneurs were given free rent for a while in some cases and other firms were given very low rents to get firms to move to Nashua and provide jobs. There was a large greeting card company at the time called Doehler Cards and Sprague Electric (made passive components like resistors and capacitors), Kaiser Electronics (construction and ship building and little car company), and Sanders Associates. There were others that I cannot remember. It is claimed that blow molding of plastics like your milk bottles was developed in one of the low rent spaces.

At Sanders Associates I worked for a man named James LeVan an M.I.T. graduate famous for making high power tubes as used in radar and electromagnetic transmission. I did basic go-for work and started to observe fascinating work being done in electronics. It was an exciting time and the Boston area was the technology center at the time much like Silicon Valley is now. Early work in printed circuits was being done at Sanders and I had the good fortune in the next summer or two to be mentored by a man named Maurice Morin who became a friend for life. He was patient with me and taught me as I helped him so I would understand the chemical processes and what we were trying to do. In the same 6th floor space was a small electro-plating laboratory that did precision plating, and a welding shop.

This was an early time and a lot was learned by experiment or what I would call whoops! learning. One day in the little office space Maurice (Mo) and I each had a desk Mo felt sick and went home. Later I did not feel so hot and figured we both had caught a "bug".

The realization that something was wrong was when I could not shut off the desk fluorescent light or the overhead fluorescent lights. Our office space was defined by 2 x 4 studs with "chicken wire" nailed to the studs to define the space. The wire was too widely knit to stop electromagnetic radiation (a Faraday shield) from penetrating and we were being "painted" by an experimental radar being tested from a nearby hill. People have been killed in similar experiences because this is much like putting a human in a large microwave oven so we were lucky. As I said these were the early days.

One of the projects that Sanders Associates won away from Kaiser Electronics in the same building was to make sonobuoys. These were fairly low cost multiple channel FM transmitters that had microphones and when they were dropped from airplanes or helicopters they would do several things like the antenna would uncurl (held in place by paper) and the microphones would drop to pre-determined depths and a dry battery that looked like a large tea bag would be activated by the salt water. The U.S. Navy decided they did not want these to be floating any longer than necessary to avoid the Russians from picking them up and learning the frequencies and therefore could jam them. Deciding how to have them sink was a challenge as sea water varies in salinity in temperature around the world. Sea water can actually remain as water until about -22°C close to an iceberg. Sonobuoys are expendable so the solution had to be low cost. The Navy wanted them to sink in a couple of hours and not float longer than 24 hours. I came up with a disc about the size of a quarter that was made from magnesium deliberately doped with nickel particles. In sea water the two elements formed a very active battery which would eat through the disc and expose a hole in the sonobuoy that a the disc covered. That went into production and I don't know what is used today. Things like this and an improved battery for the sonobuoys that I came up with were not patented as this would become public information and subject to being copied by enemies of the United States.

In between working at Sanders I believe it was the summer following the end of my junior year that I worked in the drafting area of the Davis & Furber Textile Machine Company. This company was privately owned and came out of the 19th century textile industry business. The owners were very kind and nice to me and wanted me to come work for them even after an absence of several years. The business office had the old scissor type phones out of the early 20th century and you could have made a Dickens film there with very few changes. The lead designer a Mr. Purdy was quite old and graduated from M.I.T. at the end of the 19th century. He worked at a dairy farm on the M.I.T. land to get money for school. Again, very kind and had a tremendous amount of knowledge for designing and building spinning and carding machines for wool. The foundry at the plant was based on a lot of wisdom and knowledge as they had been building some of the same equipment for decades. I did some drafting there and you may recall this was all with pen and ink drawn on a linen wax like paper and took a lot of skill and patience not to mess up. I did no design as I did not have the knowledge, but did detail drawings of parts designed by a couple of other men probably in their late 40s. Some lived in the company owned housing which they rented. Most of the summer was spent copying old drawings that had started to deteriorate with age. This was done by using a blueprint machine

One job at Sanders Associates I can recall as a low level helper was to clean the Teflon^c coated concave molds several feet in diameter where we made fiberglass-epoxy radomes for a DC-3 airplane Sanders had to test airborne radars. Unwieldy rubber gloves were used to put the fiberglass and epoxy resin in the mold and spread the resin manually. This could be done in a number of layer and usually had a plastic honeycomb shaped filler between the inner and outer layers. When the radome was complete and removed there would be some residual resin on the mold surface and it was hard to remove. You could not use metal tools to remove the resin as this would damage the mold surface so we used acetone and methyl-ethyl-ketone with soft tools and our bare hands. Sometimes I would be in the solvents up to my elbows and there was not a lot of ventilation in the area. This of course would not be allowed as the vapors were flammable and toxic, but these were the early days and we did not know any better in those times.

My last summer before graduating from L.T.I. I worked at Raytheon in Maynard, MA as a laboratory technician. One of the areas of special interest during that time was very light structures. I proposed a small radar antenna (about 12 inches in diameter) that would be made of aluminum foil and a lightweight polyurethane foam. I had developed some lightweight foams by mixing an amine into the foam mixture and placing the object in a vacuum chamber. The foil pieces were made to interlock by the model shop and stood upright in a circle. Then I poured the lightweight foam mixture in the aluminum foil voids and put the assembly in the vacuum chamber. After curing the model shop machined the radar dish by putting water in the assembly voids, freezing it, and then machining the assembly to the desired shape. It was tested on the radar range and found to work acceptably. I gave a paper on this at a student American Society of Mechanical Engineer (A.S.M.E.) meeting at M.I.T.. I do not know if this concept was used in any products, but it did get me a copy of a mechanical engineering handbook for the effort from Mr. Rogers a professor at L.T.I..

After graduation from L.T.I. in 1958 I went to work at Raytheon in Maynard, MA where they had a contract to make the bombing/navigating system for the B-58 aircraft. It was an innovative plane that was 80% bonded with adhesives and flew over 1,300 miles per hour. Raytheon in Maynard made 2 radomes of fiberglass, plastic honeycomb, and a high temperature resin. The Raytheon computer used cold cathode pentode vacuum tubes. The small team I worked on headed by "Reggie" Bullock was a very talented team and I was fortunate to learn so much at that time.

Because "Reggie" had been a non-degreed tenured professor at M.I.T. he introduced us to Professor William Murray, and others who were leaders in their field. Through "Reggie" I met Felix Zandman and Alex Redner from France who developed a process for experimental stress analysis called PhotoStress. This process I used later on the Gemini computer structure and introduced the technology to IBM.

While at Raytheon I competed for and won a year of graduate work and I chose Harvard. Dr. Bruce Chalmers world famous in metallurgy had hoped I would go for a PhD in metallurgy, but Harvard insisted on pure mathematics at that time and I was completely out of my league as my background was in engineering or applied mathematics and I did not receive my M.S. at the end of the year. Not having the money to continue studies in metallurgy I went back to work.

When the B-58 work was completed at Raytheon in Maynard the plant was closed and I went back to work at Sanders Associates and worked with Maurice Morin again. When the opportunity presented itself to go work for IBM's Federal Systems Division I went as IBM did not hire and layoff at that time like other defense contractors and with a family I wanted a more secure environment.

Chapter 2
OAO

In May 1961 I reported to IBM in Owego, N.Y. where the Federal Systems Division (FSD) was located which was only a few miles west of Endicott, N.Y. where IBM had a large manufacturing plant and a laboratory. The facility was one of several locations of FSD formed at the request of President Eisenhower to use the companies expertise in computers for federal agencies, primarily involved with but not limited to the Department of Defense (DOD). I learned from some of the people involved in the beginning that the first project was an analog gear driven bombing computer for the B-52. The design was done in temporary quarters in Vestal, N.Y. and the build of the computers was in Poughkeepsie, N.Y.. The analog computer was programmed with thumb wheels and was more than accurate enough for nuclear bomb missions.

When I arrived at the FSD facility in Owego it was comprised of a manufacturing building, two engineering buildings, and an administrative building. The population was about 5,000 people and the site was 1,600 acres in size. My assignment was in the materials engineering laboratory located in the manufacturing building. The IBM plant was different than my experience at Sanders Associates and Raytheon in the way they did business. Sanders and Raytheon were strictly DOD facilities where I worked and everything was rented or leased and a bill sent to the U.S. government every month for the buildings, equipment, and payroll. Consequently, they had little to no investment and any profit although low (1.5% to 2%) the return on investment was great.

IBM paid for everything and if defense contracts did not come in they used people and equipment to do jobs for their commercial business. This allowed them for years to have a no layoff policy and since they owned everything they did not have to get bureaucratic agencies of the Federal government to permit them to use equipment or building space. The way IBM-FSD did business was great for the taxpayer, but could be hard to compete for DOD jobs because of the return on investment (ROI) factor. IBM also had a self limit of a 10% profit maximum which could be costly on a fixed price contract (initiated by DOD Secretary McNamara). If you had problems you could lose money and at IBM if you made more than 10% profit you volunteered to give it back. IBM found out early that if you tried to give money back to the US government there was no good mechanism and it was a potential embarrassment so when that happened the agency would add to the contract giving us more to do for the money allocated. The additional work was usually some study project for future equipment.

Shortly after I arrived I was given an assignment in an area I knew little to nothing about. The company had won a contract from the young agency called the National Aeronautics and Space Administration (NASA). The contract was to build a computer for America's first telescope in space called the Orbiting Astronomical Observatory (OAO) which was to first launch in 1966. There were four launches from 1966 to 1972. See http://en.wikipedia.org/wiki/Orbiting_Astronomical_Observatory for more information.

The computer consisted of what is called cordwood modules used by a number of DOD companies at the time. Discrete components like diodes, transistors, and resistors which at that time were sealed one component at a time with axial leads (leads sticking out of each end of the component). The components were mounted between two small epoxy fiberglass boards with holes drilled in them so that when they were viewed from the side the reminded people of wood stacked thus the name cordwood. The fiberglass boards were about 1.5 inches high, 1 inch wide, and about 0.050 inches thick. When all the components were between the boards there was not a lot of room between them. A pattern had been printed on the outside of the boards and operators (usually women) would take electrical grade nickel ribbon and use a small welder with very fine tips to produce enough heat to melt the solder on the axial leads sticking through the boards which would join the leads of the components following the printed pattern on the boards. A connector was at the bottom of the cordwood module so that the module could be plugged into a large epoxy fiberglass printed circuit board (PCB).

A delicate operation was to cut the excess length of the leads with small cutters specially designed to minimize shock to the components when the cut was made. Components of that era had very delicate connections from the leads to the actual component itself. When the module was assembled and checked electrically the space between the components was filled with a special resin to keep the components from vibrating at launch and to help remove the heat. The resin was compounded by IBM to withstand 125⁰C to -55⁰C a temperature requirement by NASA. I recall an engineer named Don Smith who did much of the work on the resin.

The OAO was supposed to detect objects in space using ultraviolet wavelength light so any emissions of hydrogen from the spacecraft could mean a re-deposit of organic materials on the telescope lenses and compromise the mission. At the time of building the telescope there were a lot of guesses by scientists that the high vacuum of space would mean all organics would evaporate therefore contaminating the lenses. Other scientists said no that was not true and it was on this assumption that assembly of electronics contained a lot of organic compounds like the resin in the cordwood modules, the epoxy resin in the PCBs, and the like. IBM wanted to know what would be given off or emitted in the high vacuum of space and that was one of my first assignments. I knew nothing about high vacuum and equipment was just being developed to produce high vacuum at that time.

Since IBM had scientific resources few other companies had I first visited the IBM Yorktown Heights Watson Research Center in southern N.Y. where virtually everyone was not only a PhD but an expert in their field. I met with a man named Hollis (Holly) Caswell who was working on high vacuum equipment to produce semi-conductors in the future. At that time AT&T, Fairchild Instruments, and Texas Instruments were the industry leaders. I told him what I was trying to do and he told me about all the equipment he was using and I should get an aluminum ring with ports and a large glass bell jar. He also gave me a head start on equipment to measure high vacuum and gave some hints on how to calibrate the gauges which might shift as I did testing.

When I returned to FSD in Owego I made a list of all the equipment with prices and sketched (literally) an open aluminum frame structure to carry the equipment and small hand operated lift to raise the heavy glass bell jar to give access to the inside of the chamber. My primitive design had a small scale in it that was electronic with leads to a port in the aluminum ring and it had a small heater with a thermocouple to measure temperature. The idea was to put a small sample of the organic to be tested in the chamber and take a weight reading to start. The high vacuum would be initiated going through a start up with a "roughing" pump and then turning on the high vacuum pump and loading the cryogenic trap with liquid nitrogen. Once a high vacuum had been reached (as I recall it was close to 10^{-10} Torr.) and a weight reading had stabilized (material was being given off) I then raised the temperature to 100^0C and took another reading. When the vacuum system was turned off and back to room temperature I would take a final reading which was usually higher than the lowest weight because it would absorb moisture from the air in the normal environment. With very little trouble the system worked well after I went through a learning process.

There was some weight loss on every material but appeared to be mostly water vapor that had been absorbed in the normal environment because almost all the weight returned at the end of the test. Dow Corning predicted the weight loss on their silicone encapsulants would be water vapor. Since the telescope would be in space a short time before the lenses were exposed and their interest in proving the loss was water vapor and/or identifying anything not water vapor. I contacted the IBM Glendale analytical laboratory near us and asked if they could help. Being expert at what they did and interested in the problem a scientist there set up a gas chromatograph so it would be similar to my vacuum set up. He put samples in the vacuum chamber at his lab and analyzed the gasses emitted from the sample. As testing went along for several weeks off and on he had the tests go longer and set a clock up to turn on the analytical equipment periodically instead of running all the time. This provided excellent data to give to NASA and the experiment designers of the telescope. The Dow Corning material tested emitted mostly low molecular weight oils and not very much water and then stopped emitting once the low molecular oils boiled off. So knowing this IBM could bake the modules with the silicone materials drive off those oils thus prevent them from being emitted in space. Similar approaches were done with a few other materials that were of concern. If you look up the OAO information on the NASA or Wikipedia web sites you will find the first 2 launches were not successful as the batteries did not last long enough and the solar panels did not have enough power to keep the satellite active when in the earth's shadow. However, satellites 3 and 4 were successful and data accumulated was valuable for years.

Today it is common to put large satellites in huge vacuum chambers and apply heat to drive out undesirable materials before launch.

Chapter 3
Gemini

With President Kennedy's announcement of a goal to put a man on the moon by the end of decade (1969) NASA developed a plan to launch a man in a capsule and to orbit the earth. This was called Mercury and if you ever see a capsule at a museum you will see how small it was and how relatively primitive compared to the command module of Apollo and the Gemini two man capsule. IBM FSD was involved heavily with supplying commercial computers to NASA and contractors for doing design, calculations on orbits, ground test, and the like. IBM FSD in Owego won the contract for making the Gemini on board computer, a small keyboard to input the computer, and a read out unit. The keyboard was called the Modular Display Keyboard Unit (MDKU) and the read out unit was called the Modular Display Readout Unit (MDRU). Not too hard to understand. The MDKU was made by IBM in Owego as was the computer. The MDRU display section was sub-contracted to Lier Siegler and the rest was made by IBM. The onboard computer was to be mounted between the cockpit bulkhead and the heat shield of the capsule. The heat shield was a convex shape and would see high heat during the re-entry and dissipate the heat in addition to insulating the space between the heat shield and cockpit bulkhead. Since the heat shield was curved the computer had an odd curved shape to fit in the space. Weight was extremely important in the early space age and every effort was made to keep weight of everything at a minimum to reduce the need for more powerful rockets and/or to get more done with less weight.

A picture of the computer courtesy of the Smithsonian NASM without covers is shown here. I will call the photo below Figure 1

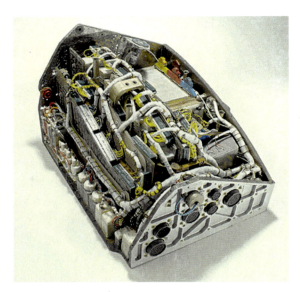

"Gemini 8 Flight, Equipment, Guidance Computer Three-quarter left side view from above of a guidance computer designed and built for Project Gemini by the Federal Systems Division of IBM. This artifact flew on the Gemini 8 mission, on March 16, 1966, piloted by astronauts Neil Armstrong and Dave Scott. Photo by Dane Penland, Smithsonian National Air and Space Museum (NASM 2005-35446)."

From http://www.ibiblio.org/apollo/Gemini.html

This is a sketch of the MDKU and MDRU to give an idea of the unit appearance. The web site does not add the unit suffix which we did at IBM.

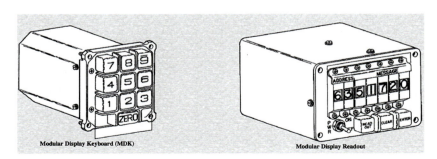

Figure 2

The chassis of the onboard computer was AZ31B magnesium with the sides machined separately and then welded together on a fixture and final machining of mounting holes and screw holes done subsequent to welding. All screw holes had steel inserts for strength and to withstand repeated screw and bolt insertion. Interestingly, IBM had the most modern numerically controlled (paper tape) machine tools available but the pieces for the chassis were done quite simply. There were not going to be a lot of these made (mission plus some for integration testing) the choice was to make steel templates which were done by skilled machinists at the Dow Chemical magnesium plant in Bay City, Michigan. The company then used a Bridgeport milling machine with a pantograph arrangement so relatively unskilled labor then just traced the pattern of the steel template (master shape) and the magnesium parts were made quite cheaply. There were four magnesium sides; the top shown in Figure 1 with the connectors, a bottom (obviously at the opposite side of the bottom, a back which is what the computer is laying on in Figure 1 and a side which is to the right. The printed circuit boards are shown vertically in Figure 1 and were multi-layer boards fairly thick and multi-layer boards were very much advanced technology during that period. The PCBs were mounted to magnesium frames considerably cut out to allow wire passage and clearance for connectors but they provide additional stiffness to the computer when it was completely assembled.

The first iteration of the computer chassis had a smaller side which would have been on the left of Figure 1. A mockup of the computer was done with dummy weights and I applied PhotoStress (remember what I learned at Raytheon) to the chassis sections in small pieces on the outside of the chassis that fit into the machined out areas. Strain gages were also applied (learned at Raytheon also). The mechanical mock up was mounted to very thick magnesium plates and were vibrated at various frequencies and with random profiles. All of this was specified by NASA based on measured and estimated vibration of launch vehicles. What I determined was the smaller side did not seem to be adding any necessary support as the loads were quite low. I thought the side could be eliminated and the thin (0.032 inch) magnesium multi-shaped cover could be extended to replace that side. In the interest of time and I guess some confidence in my findings the production chassis was drawn up that way and the cover redesigned. No testing was done to confirm the re-design as time was short and the concept was not proven until the first production model was vibrated! Needless to say no matter how sure I was it was nerve wracking for someone not even 30 years of age and a low level engineer at that. Below is a picture of a machined and welded computer chassis before final machining, surface treatment,

 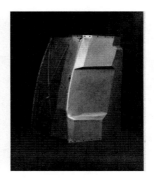

and before painting. Also a view of the complex shaped computer cover made from 0.032 inch thick AZ31B magnesium.

Above are pictures of the MDKU and MDRU with the covers off after successful mission #6. The picture of the MDKU is on the left and I will call that Figure 3 and the formed structure is made from a special magnesium alloy called LA141. The MDRU on the right is called Figure 4.

LA141 is half the weight of aluminum and about 2/3 the weight of magnesium. It is not strong but the stiffness (resistance to bending) to weight ratio is very high. In alloy naming nomenclature A is aluminum, Z is zinc, and L is lithium which is popular in batteries today because it is highly active. This activity makes it very difficult to use without corroding. Magnesium Elektron (remember the firm from my Raytheon days?) had a patent called fluoride anodizing for magnesium where a protective coating of magnesium fluoride was is formed by immersing the magnesium part in a bath of ammonium bifluoride and using a direct current to form the film. I modified the procedure for LA141 by heating the assembly made with this alloy which helped migrate the lithium (14% by weight but 50% by volume) and I then immersed it in water which reacted with the lithium leaving a magnesium rich surface which then could be made more corrosion resistant by using the fluoride anodizing process developed by Magnesium Elektron. That firm argued it was the same process since I had built on it, but IBM argued it was unique to the LA141 and other lithium rich alloys so was unique. In the end IBM obtained a patent with my name on it.

In most US corporations the patent rights for all employees have to be signed over to the company or you don't get employed. Hopefully, the employee will be rewarded. In most cases if IBM did not see a direct application to their business they published the idea which is called a defensive patent. That is that once the information is disclosed no on else can patent the idea. I had several defensive patents or publications for IBM. At IBM an employee was given points for patent disclosures if accepted. One point for a defensive publish and three points for a patent. I think it was at ten points you got a financial reward of about $2,000 and a plaque with small hanging bars to signify the individual rewards. This was called an invention plateau and very creative engineers and scientists had several invention plateaus. By the time I left IBM I had one and nearly got my second.

A lot of work was spent in the welding shop with two of the most talented welders I ever met. One was Dick Warfield who was a U.S. Navy aircraft welder and on the U.S.S. Franklin (CV/CVA/CVS-13/AVT-8) in WWII a heavily damaged aircraft carrier with a loss of 800 men. Dick was trapped beneath deck for a long time and he and another sailor used a hammer to knock on the water tight doors around them to see if there was water in them before opening. There was so much noise of metal creaking and groaning they thought they may have been sunk. Eventually they got to the top and spent the rest of the return to the mainland keeping the ship floating and under way. It really was junk Dick said, but to make it back to the mainland was a moral booster for the country at the time.

The other welder was Dominick Petrisome (sp?) was a welder at Schweizer Gliders in upper state New York before IBM. The tube frame gliders using very thin wall steel tubing took a high degree of skill to weld. He was a little younger than Dick and the three of us worked on many projects over the years to develop ways to weld LA141 and extremely thin sheets of magnesium that many in the industry said could not be done. Ask a welder if he can weld 0.010 inch thick LA141 or AZ31B with a tungsten inert gas (TIG) machine. Most would say you have to use a laser or electron beam (requires a vacuum). As you may be able to tell the people that helped me be successful were the skilled craftsmen and women on the manufacturing floor. They were an immense help in making things some thought not possible.

This may have been selfish on my part as I wanted my ideas to work and the workers got a kick out of working on new things with someone who listened to them and would see that they were rewarded. A lot of the manufacturing managers did not like this kid engineer talking to their people. I also got caught a lot putting my work ahead of the scheduled work and the workers were glad to do it because it was fun and they knew I respected their work. We all learned a lot together and did some exciting things together.

In Figure 3 (MDKU) you will note a better view of small gray colored small boxes on the top shelf (underneath the connector). These were LA141 cans with walls 0.010 inches thick. The alloy was found to have super-plasticity properties which means that at a high rate of forming it would act almost like a plastic. For example, aluminum beverage cans have been made this way for some time. A circle of aluminum alloy about 1/8 of an inch thick is put in a dye and hit with a die at a high rate of speed and the aluminum flows up the side of the die and plunger and forms the can. After forming the can, a number of operations are done to make it ready for filling, painting labels and logos, and shipping it to the beverage plant for filling and the application of a top. The forming is done so fast that it is hard to see and it may take as many as 10,000 can operations to get the die and plunger "warmed up" and ready to go.

In IBM's case we wanted to put a smaller version of the cordwood type modules described previously into these cans to make them easier to handle. The gray color is a thin polyurethane sealant over the fluoride anodize to provide corrosion protection. IBM sub-contracted the making of these cans to Zero Corporation in Detroit, Michigan the famous maker of high quality aluminum equipment, camera, and clothing cases. Zero was having problems making the parts which were being attempted in a small model type shop. Finally after a lot of talking things got desperate and a team was sent to Zero with the permission of the president of the company. When we arrived with a purchasing manager, tool and die maker, myself, and maybe someone else I cannot remember and that may have been a manufacturing representative for quantities needed. The president of the company was on vacation and the man in the model shop lacked cooperation and helpfulness to say the least. The purchasing manager, IBM legal, and the president got involved in one or more calls which resulted in us taking over the shop and the employee leaving. It took a couple of days and the tool and die man had things going well and cans were coming out well and in quantities the small Gemini program would require. If you look carefully in Figure 1 under all the white silicone coating you will see the same small cans in the computer as used in the MDKU and the MDRU. We left when things were going well and Zero employees finished the job fine.

I found an IBM newspaper clipping showing many of the key players on the Gemini program from a materials and design engineering view. Of the people shown the only one I know to be alive as I write in December 2014 is Robert Madeya who is retired and lives in New Mexico. Ray Hagstrom was a metallurgical expert, Bob Madeya a very smart organic materials engineer as was Don Smith. Hagstrom later became well known as a solder expert along with Roger Wild. One of

Personnel of Gemini Packaging (566) and Materials Engineering (580) confer on steps taken to lighten the Gemini computer structure as a result of photostress analysis. Finishing system requirements provide conductive and non-conductive surfaces. Also discussed were welded structure requirements and materials used in the manual data keyboard unit, foreground, which the astronaut will use manually to insert information into the Gemini Computer. From left, pictured are: Donald Smith, Albert White, Al Ambrose, Robert Madeya, Robert Munroe, Ray Hagstrom and Morris Wheat.

the people not mentioned above was the mechanical engineer that did all the thermal analysis and that is Bruno Pagnani. We worked together a lot and he became a lifelong friend moving to some of the same IBM-FSD facilities and our children were friends when they were young. His name will show up on the Saturn V discussion. My favorite story about Bruno on Gemini was he was asked to take a look at the estimated junction temperatures (T_J) on the Gemini power supplies. T_J is one of the best estimates of semiconductor failure rate and in general the lower the T_J the more reliable the semiconductor will be (longer life). This was a hurry up request from a manager Eric Halverson. So Bruno worked late that night and the next morning reported his work to Eric. Eric asked if this was done by computer and Bruno reported no. Eric bawled him out saying he wanted a computer analysis! Bruno was very unhappy to say the least and went to the computer area (known as Information Technology or IT today) and sat at the card punch (remember this is the old days) and punched cards reflecting all his hand work. He then fed them into the printer with the command to read and print.

The 140 column printer then printed out all of Bruno's hand input and it looked very high tech. He brought the printout to Eric later the same day and showed Eric who declared something like, "that's more like it!". Bruno then said something to the affect that it was the same information he showed in the morning and it was a damn fool that believed everything on computer printouts and left. Gotta love Bruno if you're an engineer.

As an illustration of how robust the electronic packaging was done at IBM Owego I was asked one time how would you protect the onboard computer after it lands in the ocean (think salt water and immersing your electronics). I was surprised but knowing that the capsule would be raised by crane onto the aircraft carrier typically in the landing zone that the computer should be unbolted as soon as possible and put in de-ionized or distilled water. The ship's boilers have lots of distilled water. I told them to keep immersing the computer in fresh containers (plastic trash container?) until a resistance meter (electricians have them) shows very high resistance and then put the computer in a plastic bag and put it in the ship's refrigerator not the freezer as the lower temperature will slow down any corrosive chemical reaction. After that get it to IBM Owego as soon as possible. They did all that and we put it in our large space chamber with mild heat that could pull a low vacuum to remove all the moisture from the deepest parts of the crevices in the circuit boards and modules. As a result the computers passed all the original system tests! My understanding is NASA sent them to M.I.T. Draper laboratories where they were used to develop some of the first fly by wire helicopters. I am not sure I would have wanted to fly in those test machines, but it showed how well IBM Owego built things.

In Figure 2 the copy of the MDKU and MDRU please note that the MDKU has raised walls between the keys. This was to prevent the large gloves the astronauts used from pressing two keys at once. During the Gemini period it was very slow to upload program changes by radio transmissions so the keyboard was used to make changes. The astronauts would be told or have a print out to key in a large number of digits in a controlled sequence which was time consuming and subject to error. The onboard computer on Gemini IV went into a endless loop as I recall and was draining the battery in the capsule and the computer could not be shut down although this source (http://history.nasa.gov/computers/Ch1-2.html) claims there was a power switch failure. This source claims the computer had a failure and the astronauts tried to correct it (http://www.astronautix.com/flights/gemini4.htm). In my view no one in NASA wanted to publicly review what went on in the failure analysis or to admit their own errors. The capsule had to be guided manually to a save re-entry using lines etched on the quartz viewing windows. A very sensitive job and done well by the test pilot trained astronauts (McDivitt and White)

What we saw at IBM Owego when the report came in that the onboard computer failed was everyone in the plant was called in to work even if they were not involved with the Gemini program. IBM Corporate had taken a full page ad in the Wall Street Journal celebrating IBM's participation and it could not be cancelled after the news of the alleged failure was announced.

Tom Watson, Jr was the CEO and wanted every effort put forth to find the source of the problem. IBM engineers were already talking about an incorrect input by astronauts using the MDKU. NASA thought a relay had "stuck" causing the power drain. The relays used were sealed gold contact relays with multiple contacts (in case one failed). Relays were slammed, shaken, overheated, and generally abused and the only way one could be made to stay shut when it should return to an open position was by welding the contacts using a laser! The onboard computer design was by NASA and had no provision to stop power going to it and running the capsule battery down if there was an incorrect program input or other type of failure. Tom Watson, Jr ordered an on/off provision be immediately implemented on the computer which was a relatively easy job for the engineers, but this was not authorized by NASA. He even ordered the computers in the government bonded storage area be removed and the change be put in which was unheard of because they at that point had been accepted and were government property. When he was told the IBMers could not do that the question was asked it is told, "Who do you work for them or me?". The changes were put in on all computers built and the few future ones to be built. In the end NASA concurred and everyone was advised not to mention the suspected real fault which was likely an astronaut error (could have been caused by those huge gloves even with the guards on the MDKU). Even the web sources today generally say there was a computer failure, but they differ in accounts. To my knowledge there was never an official failure report published by IBM. Better to keep things quiet and not embarrass the customer.

One reason at least one source cites for the selection of IBM for the Gemini onboard computer was the type of core memory used on OAO which worked very well and the core memory is still the most reliable in space to resist radiation (mostly cosmic rays). The core memory of this type was an IBM invention and consisted of two holes in an oval core and it has five wires threaded through the cores. This gave a read/write capability that was non-destructive. All other ferrite core memories were a read and re-write type with four wires. In the commercial production the cores were a little larger and a machine did the wiring automatically (quite a machine) and if the thin copper wire broke it was welded together and the wiring continued. NASA wanted no welding and the five wires that went through the 4096 core plane memory should be perfect. Since the cores were smaller the 4096 cores had to be hand threaded with the five wires with no breaks! This was done by only a few women that could do it and it was very frustrating to work under a microscope with the requirements and not go "crazy". There was a lot of frustration. When some astronauts visited the plant (Grissom, Chaffee, and White I think) they were toured through the manufacturing floor by IBM executives. When one of the astronauts saw what the women were doing and asked, "Do you do that all day?" a well experienced assembler ("Hoot" Gibson) said "all f___ day!"). The astronauts laughed as they understood. The proper IBM executives were non-plussed and after leaving told the IBM Owego manufacturing management they wanted her fired. The Owego managers told them that was not going to happen as she was an excellent worker and was about 1/3 of the production capability for Gemini core mats. However, they did build the women working on the core memories a raised floor glassed in area where they could play music (again unheard of in IBM at the time). People could look and wonder but no conversation with outsiders was going to be had.

After core mats were wired they were encapsulated so a special silicone resin could be applied which when molded resulted in a number of round flat bumps slightly raised from the flat resin. The concept was that when a number of core planes were put one on top of the other the round bumps would make a gentle contact with each other.

A photo of an encapsulated area is shown below which was copied from http://www.cedmagic.com/history/whirlwind-core-memory.html

When a number of core arrays were stacked on top of each other (39 of them I believe) it made a memory of 159,744 bits. The ends of each gold plated tabs were bent so that they made contact with the tab on the next array below it. The whole assembly was then put in a chamber and the contacts welded using an electron beam aimed at the top array and the beam consequently welded all the tabs below it. This was a process developed by the commercial arm of IBM.

A story I suspect that cost IBM a lot of money (not reimbursed by the government) was the memory array contamination problem found in the silicone gel molding compound. As production increased very small black particles started showing up on the microscopic examination of the final product. It was feared that these black particles were fragments of pieces broken off the ferrite cores which were black in color. Even if the memory array seemed to work fine this suspected damage might cause one or more individual cores

to fail. With a great deal of difficulty some of the very fine particles were removed from the contaminated arrays without knowingly damaging the cores themselves. This was tedious and difficult but when a very small group of particles were gathered so that they consisted of enough to analyze it was found that the particles were not from the cores. The particles seemed to be organic in nature. More particles were gathered from defective arrays that were showing up now and again. It was mysterious and casting a pall over the memory assembly and manufacturing process. Finally enough particles were gathered and subjected to the best organic testing we had at the time which I believe was infra-red spectrography. A print out of the spectra obtained was then compared with known organic compounds in large reference books kept in the laboratory. No computer programs existed at the time that would do the comparison and it depended on the expertise of the testing engineers who were very good. No luck on comparisons with many hours spent trying. Bruno Pagnani and I decided to go to the manufacturing floor and watch the assembly operation of the memory arrays from start to finish. Several days and nights were spent without result until one night I noticed an operator doing something that until recently was never allowed and that was to eat snacks at their work station. IBM had even installed vending machines on the manufacturing floor for the convenience of the employees. I went to a machine, bought a package of Oreo cookies and the next morning brought them to the analytical lab and they tested the black cookies. Sure enough it was a perfect match! Immediately the management forbid eating at the work stations. After the visit by the astronauts described previously the move to a special area glassed in and no eating allowed at the work stations solved both the contamination and embarrassment issue. The workers could take breaks outside of their work area and once they knew of the potential contamination of the arrays were very careful to wash their hands and not introduce by accident anything that did not belong in the array. Bob Christiansen and others solved other issues early in the silicone gel encapsulation of the wired arrays, but that is what I remember and the production was tedious, but went well after the ones I was aware of and have written about.

The experience on the Gemini program with the difficult to work with magnesium lithium alloy LA141 and the more typical AZ31B and seldom used HK31A would be pushed to the limit on the upcoming Saturn V program.

You may enjoy this side story. At this time in the 1960s people in banks and insurance companies were producing computer printouts that ran hundreds of pages and auditors brought up in the eye shade accounting environment rarely detected fraud. We had a CPA who has a good computer programming background in FSD and IBM Corporate grabbed him to start working for them and help the commercial honest financial people detect fraud in their firms. He was Walter Stuhldreher the nephew of one of the famous Notre Dame legendary four horseman and he was just as big in size. Hard man to argue with.

Chapter 4
MMRBM

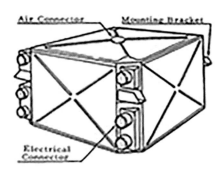

IBM had designed and developed the Titan III nuclear ballistic missile guidance computer or at least the last series of them. This was before I joined IBM. The technology was a rotating drum memory which spun on air bearings. The electronic packaging was cordwood modules as described in Chapter 2. The rocket was a very thin skin rocket which required pressure inside to hold it rigid. The fuel mixture had an oxidizer nitrogen tetroxide which was extremely corrosive as well as toxic and a vicious oxidizer. The aluminum frame was covered with panels made from a gold plated metal skin on top of a epoxy fiberglass material as I recall. The gold was necessary because fuel could leak on the computer and if it did without a gold protective surface the fuel would eat through the metal and into the computer. From http://en.wikipedia.org/wiki/ASC-15 a sketch of the computer is shown above as Figure 1.
The photo on the above right is the aluminum chassis called Figure 2.

This type of spinning drum memory was used for the Titan III by extending the length of the drum for more memory. The design of this computer and the length of time it was used including the Saturn IC rocket is a testament to the design team and especially materials work done by IBM Endicott to plate the nickel-cobalt alloy on the drum. Although the plating was done in Owego the technology came from Endicott who developed it for commercial computers and were beat out by a renegade team at the new plant in San Jose, California. The IBM San Jose team developed disk memories and that technology has been used for years by many companies and increased in memory density to almost unbelievable levels.

I start this chapter to show there was a history at IBM Owego in the area of computers for rockets with their very high severe vibration environments. The federal government decided that they needed an answer to what they believed the Russians were doing which was to mount intercontinental ballistic missiles (ICBMs) on railroad cars so they could be moved around and hard to defeat. These missiles were long enough to reach western Europe (our allies) and some parts of the US. So having a considerable but shorter range than the ICBMs in the arsenals of both countries the new ones were called Mobile Medium Range Ballistic Missiles or MMRBMs. IBM Owego was asked to bid on a guidance computer for this kind of missile and I was part of the team. The vibration environment was severe as usual so I had looked at Lord Rubber Company's viscoelastic vibration dampers and suggested that the same material be used as part of the computer's "skin" or covers to help with the damping. A mockup was made on an accelerated schedule and I applied the PhotoStress material to the covers which were an integral part of the structure. The schedule was intense and we assembled one night to put the mockup structure in vibration testing to assess the design. The only test area available was a small area where the seismic mass (granite slab weighing tons sitting on steel I-beams) was very close to one wall opposite the control room. In order to measure the strains on the structure I would have to get between the vibration table with seismic mass and the wall with my synchronized polarized light. I was a lot thinner then! Part of the testing to to go through the test spectrum at very low levels to "tune" the electromagnetic shaker. The operator started the routine and I was looking through the polarizer when I felt strong pressure on my mid-section. Looking down the I-beams had gone into resonance and were bending like plastic! You study this in school but seeing I-beams like that bending as they were did not look real. It was real and the granite slab had "floated" off the I-beams and were trying to push me through the wall. I yelled and they cut the power. I was pinned and could not get out as much as I wanted to. Jim Price went into the control room and looked at the paper record of the "tune" run and the decision was to go back to the low frequency where the resonance occurred and apply the lowest power possible. It should work. I sure hoped so. The operator did what Jim suggested and I pushed the whole granite slab easily back to its place and power was cut. Jim made the decision not to "tune" that low in frequency which was below our test frequency anyway and after a short break (think I had to go to the rest room) we did the testing. The structure looked like it would work well.

Another company "won" the bid and in the end the whole program was eliminated by the U.S.. I say won because IBM was so good at that point that often our regional congressman would call and say that some committee gave a contract to someone else because "it was their turn". We always spent a lot of effort on honest bids and although we were not the only smart people in the business we were way above average and if we knew there were going to be turns we would not have tried so hard. Seemed like a rigged game. But that is what pork is in the DOD business and other agencies too.

Chapter 5
Saturn V

I think my first contact with the potential involvement of IBM FSD with the Saturn V guidance program was about the middle of 1963. IBM had been involved with NASA rocket guidance with a modified Titan III (ASC-15) rotating magnetic drum computer used on Saturn SA-6 and I was not involved. I was working on OAO at the time. For background on the Saturn program and the effort to get a man on the moon see the following which are only a few of the many web resources available.

http://en.wikipedia.org/wiki/Saturn_%28rocket_family%29

http://en.wikipedia.org/wiki/Saturn_V

http://en.wikipedia.org/wiki/Saturn_V

The LVDC and LVDA shown on the Instrument Unit (IU) at the Space Museum in Huntsville, AL is the best display of the Saturn V and the IU in the country in my opinion.

NASA had used IUs on various rockets and it was a short (about 4 feet for Saturn V) and approximately 33 feet in diameter. The structure was a honeycomb structure that I believe was made of titanium and supplied by Boeing as a subcontractor to IBM after they won the contract to integrate the IU with all its equipment and to build three major components. They were the Launch Vehicle Digital Computer

(LVDC), the Launch Vehicle Data Adapter (LVDA), and the Saturn Switch Selector (SSS) (built by IBM after some one else failed).

The IU had a number of "cold plates" with a grid array of mounting holes that equipment could be bolted to. The cold plates were made of aluminum and had coolant pumped through them to keep equipment cooled. Cooling was provided by an evaporative cooler which was a porous nickel I think and liquid was evaporated from it which lowered the temperature and the coolant flowing through the evaporator in sealed lines would be cooled. This cooling system for equipment that required cooling was convenient since all types of electronics in their boxes could be designed to fit on the grid of mounting holes. However, these cold plates took a lot of room on the inner periphery of the IU and although versatile were not space efficient.

I flew to Huntsville, Alabama where the Marshall Space Flight Center (MSFC) was located on the U.S. Army Missile Command base. IBM people escorted me to the MSFC to meet with NASA personnel to see a mockup of the Instrument Unit (IU) proposed for the Saturn V series of rockets. One of the NASA men I met was von Haeussermann who was in charge of guidance. Another was Wilhelm Angele (flat cable inventor). I was told that a problem to be solved was there was not enough room for all the cables running between equipment and to radio transmitters to provide information to the ground (telemetry). Another problem was when estimates of all the equipment were made there was not enough room on the cold plates for all the equipment.

IBM engineers had some advanced ideas to design a LVDC. Most of the components would be hybrid circuits which would be made on small ceramic substrates called Unit Logic Devices (ULDs) surface mounted to multi-layer PCBs. Some pictures can be found on several web sites but this one also shows the ferrite core memory core stacks.
http://www.vintchip.com/MAINFRAME/NASALVDC/APOLLOLVDC.html

I cannot remember all the very smart engineers on the design, but they were the usual team assembled for the most challenging projects. I know Don Buckley was on the lead engineers on the multi-layer PCBs, Ralph Jackson on packaging, Charlie Packard on component engineering, Bruno Pagnani on thermal analysis, Jim Price the electronic packaging 2nd level manager, Jack Kracke mechanical engineer, Dan Vullemier a packaging manager, "Dusty" Panaro a packaging manager, a great support team in developing automatic wiring programs which were used to route most wires on the multi-layer PCBs and final wiring completion was done manually. I was in a support role to the electronic packaging team and spent a lot of time with Jim Price and his team. When an estimate was made of the size of the LVDC and LVDA with the circuits available at that time it was clear that the boxes would be basically "two story". That means that for the area allowed in the IU we could not get everything in that area unless the units were a double level. This was a problem because to cool the electronics a preliminary thermal analysis showed the logic level (top) could not be cooled adequately as the heavy dual redundant core memory stacks would be on the level closest to the IU wall. Please remember the units would be mounted to the walls and the heaviest mass should be closest to the wall for structural support. Somewhere along the line I suggested we use LA141 as the structure and bore cooling holes through the walls and circulate the coolant where it would do the most good and we would eliminate the need for more cold plates when there really was not enough room for more. A similar cooling scheme could be used for the LVDA which had a number of power supplies since this unit was a large digital to analog and analog to digital box.

After discussion with the head of engineering Monroe Dickinson, the plant manager Art Cooper, and several FSD marketing people it was decided to respond to the NASA request for proposal with integrally cooled IBM units which would save NASA precious cold plate space (they did not have). I can recall that just before I was to enter the plant manager's office I was approached by an IBM Corporate Vice President Bob Ellsworth. Evidently he had been told by some of the engineers in the commercial arm of IBM or someone in FSD marketing that the bid might not be in conformance with the NASA request for proposal (RFP) because the units would not be cold plate mounted. The wording in the RFP was ambiguous and did not require cold plate cooling as far as we had determined. Ellsworth (brother-in-law of CEO Thomas Watson, Jr) told me I should suggest we could go in Cooper's office and say that we should change the response to cold plate cooling and then after we won the contract tell NASA we needed to make an engineering change and go to integral cooling. Evidently someone feared we would lose the contract by bidding integral cooling. Winning the LVDC, LVDA, and integration of the IU was important in money and prestige for IBM. IBM as a corporation would stand to sell commercial computers for ground support and simulation easier if they had the IBM FSD win. I was non-plussed that he thought a low level guy like me could change the team decision and did not know what to say for a moment. I then told me that IBM did not pay me enough to lie, cheat, and steal. I did this because I thought to knowingly tell NASA we could make the requirements of the RFP and know that we could not was deception which was wrong with the stated principles of IBM ethics, but also in violation of business ethics. I walked past him into Cooper's office and we had the short meeting and agreed to bid with integral cooling which would be an industry first for any computer known and Ellsworth never said a word. We won and the NASA leadership at MSFC (most were Panemaunde veterans of V2 fame we had spirited to the US ahead of the Russians) said that is exactly the type of solution they had in mind. Creative, solved the IU space problem, and they knew IBM would find a way. We did not hear a word about cooling issues from the corporate arm of IBM until later.

So since I was the guy who came up with the idea of putting holes through the walls of the computer I was the one who had to help execute this in manufacturing. I had my bright idea knowing that rifles had been drilled the length of the barrel for years. My first trip was to Ithaca Gun which was right up the road. They made shotguns and some small caliber rifles. When the kind people at Ithaca asked what I wanted to see was I told them I wanted to see how they drilled the holes in the rifles. Off we went to the manufacturing floor and much to my horror I found out that the industry had morphed to spinning the barrel at very high speeds and the drill was stationary.

We could not spin the very large billets of LA141 so I asked if there were any machines that spun the drills and the answer was not that they knew of. You can hardly imagine how I felt at that point. So after recovering from that blow I decided to go to the IBM Endicott machine floor since the men on the IBM Owego manufacturing floor did not know about a machine that could drill holes about 24 inches long with accuracy. When I asked in IBM Endicott (remember IBM had a lot of electro-mechanical systems and had some skilled machinists) if they knew of a machine that could do the drilling we required. And the answer was sure and led me to the area where they were drilling hinges that had to be 6 feet long! I asked them why they were doing that and the answer was that when people paid the money they were for IBM computers the cabinet doors better open smoothly and perfectly. So I found out that Brown and Sharpe machine tools in Providence, Rhode Island made the machine. I started having some real hope at that point and when I brought the information back to the machine floor at IBM Owego they had Brown and Sharpe come in for a talk. The discussion went well and the decision was made after the solid LA141 billets were rough machined for the pages the billets would be sent to Rhode Island for drilling.

Top view showing page slots

Bottom Side Fluoride Anodized and Painted

Side View Showing Cooling Holes and Legs Welded on

Bottom side in process of machining

LVDA Main Frame Machined

Painted LVDC DeepCover to Clear Memory Stacks

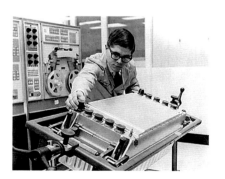
LVDC in NASA White Being Readied for Test

Page cartoon showing ULDs partially machine mounted to the Multi-layer PCB adhesive bonded to a frame of AZ31B or LA141 dependent on thermal load

Pages were located in the machined slots in the LVDC frame and attached with small bolts aligned with the connectors in the multi-layer PCB covering the bottom middle of the LVDC. Note that in the EE Times article in the reference section it states that in 1965 plated through holes were not available and that is not true for PCBs as all the pages and backplane had plated through holes. Perhaps the author was talking about ceramics, but it is not clear. This large board was called a back plane. The CPU was triple redundant and "voted" before executing an operation. Any failures would be recorded and sent to the ground by telemetry. At least one LVDC was run continuously for 10 years at the MSFC and never had a simplex failure. The memories were dual redundant ferrite core memories similar to the read-write non-destruct ferrite core type. I have several references at the end of this chapter which will explain more about the LVDC, LVDA, SSS, and the IU.

One major milestone I had to achieve was to work with the Brooks and Perkins foundry making the very reactive LA141 billets so that when machined no repairs would have to be made to close small holes in the coolant paths caused by flux inclusions. No one had made billets this large using this alloy with such demanding void requirements. Once we knew we were going to be working with large billets I interfaced with the non-destructive inspection people and got them samples to calibrate their x-ray machine and I helped them convince management we need an oil bath ultrasonic tester that had very fine resolution to find defects in thinner pieces of LA141. The x-ray machine was modern but did not have enough resolution to find the fine voids we were trying to detect and reject the billets of material before machining started.

Then I found in a magazine article that Philips in the Netherlands had a laboratory model x-ray that was better than anything else on the market. No models were for sale as this was a development model. I went to Art Cooper the plant manager and told him about it and we really needed to get one of those if we could. Art called the head of Philips directly and convinced him to ship us the laboratory model to aid the space program. It happened! That was just one example of how IBM FSD would provide the tools and resources to make things happen if you had a good case and was credible. There was no limit. It was amazing and the machine was delivered to the non-destructive test area.

We were machining LA141 billets after examining them with the tools we had and even when we thought we had good ones after finish machining when they were leak tested with argon (helium was too small) there would be small leaks which would have to be repaired by welding. This was acceptable for development models but not flight. Each billet was numbered and Brooks and Perkins was making progress on this difficult metal and I was asked by Monroe Dickinson what number billet would I predict no leaks. From the best estimate I had at the time I said number 35 (all billets were serialized but not used and rejects were sent back to Brooks and Perkins). Dickinson said very seriously that better be right as my job and his depended on it. Luckily number 35 went through all tests without repairs and others followed. The Philips x-ray machine that had been rushed to us really helped along with the skilled technicians in the non-destructive test area.

In parallel with all the work on the materials work for the LVDC and LVDA including staying close to manufacturing to help resolve problems when they arose I got to learn a something about making the small ceramic hybrid circuits that went into the electronics. The alumina substrates were printed using silk screen technology (stainless steel screens) to deposit gold-palladium material to make circuit lines. The substrates were fired in continuous belt ovens at about 850°C after a short dry cycle. Resistors consisting of ruthenium oxide (important point later) were screened and fired on the bottom. The semiconductors were the same size with three nickel plated copper balls solder coated that provided the interconnection between the die and top circuit lines of the substrate which were solder coated. The semiconductors were bipolar and either a single transistor or a dual diode. After performing the necessary processing to make the transistor or diode the wafer was sputtered with pure silicon and then subjected to steam in a unique process to IBM which made an impervious quartz passivation layer. Holes were etched in the layer to provide access to the contact for the small plated ball and the solder was melted in a hydrogen atmosphere to make a solder joint. After dicing the small chips were tested at a very high rate of speed and the die were hand placed on ULDs. When the technology was transferred to IBM Poughkeepsie for production of commercial computers the substrates were larger and the die placement automatic. The EE Times article in the reference section claims the small ceramic cover adhesively bonded over the die on the top surface of the ULD made a hermetic seal. This is not true and I never said that. The die had a small coating of silicone gel over them but the cover provided protection from mechanical damage. I used to say it kept the dogs and cats out meaning it was not for environmental (humidity or gasses) protection which was provided by the quartz surface on the die. That surface protection is why IBM had such good reliability at low cost while the industry was going to integrated circuits and hermetic packages.

When the small pre-production development line was transferred from Owego to Poughkeepsie a number of problems surfaced as production ramped up to make quantities to be delivered to IBM Owego for the Saturn V program. One of the problems was contamination on the ceramic substrates that prevented good bonding of the protective cap. Another was missing die and chipped or damaged die. I was asked to go to Poughkeepsie to help solve the problems as a young engineer and frankly no one else wanted to go. I had two pre-school children at home and leaving every Sunday to drive to Poughkeepsie and work all week and return on Friday night was especially on my wife "Dottie" as we had 2 pre-school children at the time. I did this commute in a rental car as we only had one car and Dottie could not be left stranded. During the week I stayed at a motel. I did this for 6 months.

I found in that summer (1963 I think) the Poughkeepsie people did not welcome me watching what was going on and reporting faults. The first problem to attach was the contamination issue. I was used to UV or "black light" portable units in Owego to help find organic contamination which would glow in the dark when the light was shined on something. Poughkeepsie had no UV lights so I borrowed one from the non-destructive test people in Owego and tried to examine different pieces of tooling used in the assembly process. I asked for a room that was completely dark and they said there was none available. So I set my little inspection station up in the men's restroom and shut the lights off. I found contamination on the tools used to hold substrates. Taking a tool with me to Owego (Poughkeepsie did not like that) the contamination was from the silicone gel. The gel would deter bonding with the epoxy adhesive and so once the contamination was identified the tooling was cleaned when Owego management put the pressure on. Not popular incident number one.

I then set about trying to find why die were missing after assembly or were damaged. Poughkeepsie was not going to waste precious resources on FSD when the System 360 project was started. I noticed that many of the untrained young women were wearing bracelets. As they moved their hands around the bracelet chains or the bracelets were hitting the die and damaging them or knocking them off position before soldering would "lock" them in place. The jewelry would have to come off I reported to Owego who notified the Poughkeepsie management. Not popular number two.

The production people in Poughkeepsie had complained that all the overtime (coupled with System 360 overtime) was taking a toll and so they took off for two weeks. We thought this was laughable since extended hours were regularly worked by many of us in FSD. In any case I wanted to try soldering tests on the substrates which had a lower than expected yield. I brought a soldering pot and flux from Owego to Poughkeepsie but no one was on the floor and no 220V source was available to power the solder pot. So I opened up the power box on a Bridgeport milling machine in the model shop and tapped into the 220V line and did my experiments but got detected doing this before I was finished. I had found more contamination on the substrates inhibiting good solder covering. Reported that again. Not popular number three.

During my commuting to Poughkeepsie I was often accompanied by a manager from the purchasing area that was responsible for getting the management in charge of making the parts for IBM Owego. He was great and I cannot remember his name. On the Poughkeepsie side I recall a tooling manager (George Nagy) who led a very imaginative and conscientious team who did great work on the ULDs but outside of that team most of the management was contentious and should have expended their energy solving the problems. The overall head of the newly formed Components Division was Ed Davis and I don't recall meeting him, but allegedly they heard about this young upstart from Owego. During all my commuting time it was summer and very hard on my wife and children as I was not there for the better part of several months. At the end of something like 4 months or so I was asked to continue my "good work" at Poughkeepsie and I said no. There were others that could do that to help who never showed up, and it was too hard on my family. At that point the FSD management that had been so tight with the money about where I stayed and the sacrifice my family had made offered an apartment with a swimming pool, access to a local country club for the family, and some other perks. I still said no and it would have been nice to have that offer during the summer but the swimming pool and winter in Poughkeepsie was not an attraction. That is when the Components Division made an offer to FSD Owego to hire me. I didn't go and to this day don't know if that was a missed opportunity or an effort to get me in their organization to stop me from finding embarrassing problems.

If you care to examine the cross section of an ULD on page 2 of the EE Times article you will see the S shaped clips that held the ULD and served as a contact between the top and bottom circuit lines as well as providing compliance during the wide variations in temperature the NASA specifications required even though the equipment would have experience a much smaller temperature range in practice. What is not as obvious is every connection was redundant with a very small C shaped clip in addition to the S shaped clip. This was done because the ceramic has a very small thermal expansion coefficient compared to the copper and the dual redundancy ensured that the connection from the top to the bottom of the substrate would remain reliable. The S shape clip allowed compliance as the multi-layer PCB connection would also expand more than the ceramic. Equal force equations were developed to estimate the combined thermal expansion of the magnesium or magnesium-lithium page frames. Those estimates were used to calculate the strain movement on the clips and much experimental work was done in this area. NASA required DOD type of thermal cycling of the pages with components mounted to ensure no failures. As I recall the temperature range was -40°C to +125°C at a rate of 2 cycles per hour with dwells of 10 minutes a the minimum and maximum temperatures. This was a tough test as the solder was allowed to creep and cause ratcheting to failure. IBM used a 2% silver solder on the joints for clips on the ceramic and for the attachment to the multi-layer PCBs. Temperature-humidity testing was done to make sure there was no silver migration.

It is hard to describe how much basic solder work was done by IBM Owego and Worcester Polytechnic Institute hired by IBM. Long term creep studies were done as well as intermetallic studies to measure growth and to find the optimum thickness of nickel on the copper to deter unwanted brittle intermetallics from forming. Roger Wild, Frank Ripp, and Ray Hagstrom were the key investigators. Their work resulted in the development of tooling which was made into production tools by the George Nagy Poughkeepsie team. That tooling held the S and C clips off the substrates so that the optimum thickness of solder joint would be formed for optimum reliability.

The thickness of solder on the multi-layer PCBs when the ULDs were joined was controlled by the amount of solder screened on the PCBs. All of this work took considerable effort and was not recognized for some time until a number of technical papers were written and IBM Owego became nationally known for its basic solder work with relation to thermal fatigue. This work was further advanced when the IBM Components Division paid IBM FSD in Owego to do long term testing at various temperature rates and number of cycles per day. This work went on for several years to expand the data base already done by the IBM Components Division in support of its flip chip technology.

As you can imagine with such a major undertaking there was a lot of parallel work going on with the new technology being introduced. Bruno Pagnani was the leader in doing the thermal analysis and others made mockups or thermal dummies of the LVDC and LVDA to verify the modeling done by Bruno. Silicone patches with heater wires were bonded to areas that would have electronics; power supplies, logic pages, memories with electronics, the analog to digital (A/D), and digital to analog (D/A) converters. Controls were on hand to change the thermal loads as appropriate as sometimes circuit designers would under-estimate the original power loads. A number of thermal runs were made that verified the soundness of the thermal design. Some time later when a working LVDC and LVDA were available thermocouples were placed where the most power dissipation was located and NASA was very pleased with the results which would mean by running very conservative temperatures the equipment would be very reliable.

As I stated elsewhere an engineering estimate had to be made of the resultant thermal expansion of the page assembly when the MLBs with ULDs were bonded to the page frame. The expansion would be different for AZ31B magnesium than LA141 magnesium Lithium. This was quite a complex multi-material mix and had to include the adhesive used to bond the MLB to the page frame. Bruno and I worked on that very hard for several days and nights trying different approaches. Ron Tomeck a fellow engineer went home every night on time which did not sit well with me. One evening as he was leaving he said he would work on the problem the next day. Bruno and I came up with a reasonable estimate and declared victory, but Bruno told me not to say anything to Ron. I said yeh. The next morning when Tomeck hit the door I told him not to bother we had solved it. I thought Bruno would kill me! Thank goodness he was a friend, but he still reminds me of it and that was 50 years ago!

Success? Well not is all it seems. The newly formed Component Division was having trouble delivering enough components for the LVDC and LVDA. They were under a lot of pressure to produce enough Solid Logic Technology (SLT) modules which were similar to the IBM FSD components (ULDs) and were not putting as much talent and effort into the FSD needs. In a typical political ploy the Components Division had the Yorktown Research Center evaluate the LVDC thermal design and found a PhD who opined that the LVDC would "burn up". FSD's response was it worked fine and NASA had approved the testing of the real equipment. Bruno Pagnani wanted to know what the name was of the PhD who had maligned him by saying his analysis was faulty. He was steaming mad and as an ex-wrestler in the NCAA and guard on the Lehigh University football team he wanted to meet that blankety blank jerk, but no one would give him the PhD's name. The PhD stayed in IBM for years playing the part of a thermal analyst. Bruno at that point had a Masters of Science degree in mechanical engineering and decided to go back to school and get his PhD. I asked what problems could he solve as a PhD that he could not solve now. His answer was "I am never going to get out degreed again." In IBM like so many other big companies the higher degrees and more widely known schools counted more than individual contribution since a lot of the management had insufficient talent for evaluating technology contributions.

As an aside I have the 2 volumes of the books called "The Design of Early IBM Computers" by the MIT press which was authorized by IBM. In it they describe two relevant things to this discussion. One was the highly political atmosphere in IBM dominated by sales and marketing people not technology people. The other was that IBM only introduced one new basic technology in the computer industry up to the writings of the books which went into the 1970s. That one new thing was the disk drive developed in San Jose, California. For several years the older more political IBM location in Endicott pushed the rotating drum memory. Interestingly, that location refused direct orders by Thomas Watson, Jr the CEO and head of engineering to develop an electronic computer which was being done by competitors. He was so frustrated at one point he took every electrical engineer hired by the company and moved them to Poughkeepsie and gave them the charter because he could not get the highly political Endicott to perform.

So how did IBM perform so well in the commercial computer market? The technologists were great and had every kind of technology one could think of in a laboratory, but the sales marketing dominated management had no system to choose "the next best thing". Once some competitor came out with a product, IBM would pull something equal to or better out of a laboratory somewhere and with its superior manufacturing capability would go market it and dominate. I remember years after I left FSD that I saw small color ink jet printers at the Boulder laboratory and asked why we had not gone after the market that Canon ended up dominating. The answer was that the marketing decision was there must be no need for color printers because no one else was making one!

Back to Saturn V. One of the things I had done was to have the machine floor make me several tubes of LA141 by drilling holes through the material and then turning them to make tubes. I linked a number of them together with plastic hose and hose clamps and used a 12 volt automobile gasoline pump to circulate the NASA stipulated IU coolant which had some methanol in it (therefore the gasoline pump). I had the shop make up a stainless steel tank of about 5 gallons and ran the fluid in a loop through the tubing. Every couple of months I would stop the system and examine the inside of the tubing walls which showed some corrosion film, but none of the tubing leaked. The walls were about 1/8 inch thick as I recall. When I asked NASA how long they expected for the exposure of the coolant to the LVDC and LVDA they had to think some (remember most other equipment was on cold plates and not exposed to the coolant) they said 500 hours. That was not in the specifications in the contract. I thought from my experience that the exposure might be more like 5,000 hours and that was the target I used. In reality I ran my small experiment for over a year (about 8,000 hours) and did not have a problem. I changed the coolant periodically since any minor corrosion tends to buffer the solution and reduce the corrosion rate.

A year or more after flights were made with the LVDC and LVDA some of the production equipment would not pass electrical test. The components reliability laboratory at FSD Owego (Chuck Packard) found that hydrogen produced by the minor corrosion of the LA141 material was reducing the resistors and changing the resistance. This could be reversed by purging the equipment by blowing dry clean air into them. At first puzzled we found that the Components Division had changed the resistor material from Ruthenium Oxide to Palladium Oxide because the latter was cheaper and used in the commercial SLT modules. This was approved by the electrical team at FSD Owego as it seemed to be a logical change. Palladium Oxide resistors could not be just as resistant to resistance change with a small concentration of hydrogen as the Ruthenium Oxide resistors. However, talking to DuPont (supplier of both materials) the Components Division used a very small amount of Palladium which made them more sensitive (lower activation energy to change). We had used Ruthenium Oxide resistors (higher activation energy to change) in FSD Owego developing the ULDs so had not seen this problem. In any case routine purging of the air in the production boxes in storage was done (weekly I think) to ensure no problems would occur. Most of the times the equipment would be stored with the coolant inside the walls of the equipment as they had a special fluid disconnect which would allow coolant lines to be attached and removed with no fluid being lost or air introduced (which would lower the heat transfer coefficient).

In addition to thermal testing of the LVDC and LVDA and the obvious electrical testing over a wide temperature range, units were vibration tested and shock tested. Vibration tested showed that the LA141 material's dampening properties were advantageous on such a large unit. Thermal cycling of pages made of LA141 and AZ31 using test ULDs (thermal continuity samples) showed the superior compliance of the FSD designed S shaped clips and the controlled height solder joints. This kind of information was used for later technology parts that were soldered to the surface of MLBs (surface mount technology), and people like Roger Wild and Ray Hagstrom became know nationally and internationally for this work and many companies copied it. Roger used to give courses through the American Society of Metals (ASM) long after he retired.

I have three other stories regarding my career at a personal level regarding my work as part of a large team on the Saturn V LVDC and LVDA. I have to emphasize team because I had an idea which mechanical designers turned into drawings, computer controlled machining experts put into methods on how to machine this difficult metal, skilled welders were able to do their work to add the mounting legs and seal the cooling passage, non-destructive test technicians worked to help find any faults that would cause leaks or weakness, and above all the support of Jim Price, Monroe Dickinson, and Art Cooper who provided all the resources we needed as a team to make it happen. Not many young engineers or engineers at any age have this kind of support and their ideas do not come to fruition.

One story is about my immediate management and our conflict. In IBM there are levels of management and formally my immediate manager was a very nice man but not very good manager named George Thomas. His manager was named Jack Goetz and he was a components manager. He reported to Monroe Dickinson who reported to Art Cooper the plant manager. On Saturn V like Gemini and MMRBM I was in support of and spent a lot of time with Jim Price's team that had the responsibility for designing the boxes and how all the electronics in the boxes would fit. Evidently my integral support of the Jim Price team was welcomed but not historically how things worked in Owego. The old way was the equipment design people did the design without a lot of help from the materials engineering people although there were some exceptions like plastic encapsulants and failure analysis of materials. After the Saturn V equipment successfully passed NASA qualification and was deemed ready for flights it was time for my performance rating and George

Thomas marked me as satisfactory (mediocre rating) and when I protested he said I was always off helping those design people and was not working in his department like I should be. He did not see the big picture that IBM Owego was successful on an important project and we did it by working in a cross organizational way not a vertical way. Being very upset (strong headed?) I went to Monroe Dickinson's office after stopping by Jim Price's office and told them I was not going to work with them again after getting a performance rating like that from my manager. Dickinson listened and told me to calm down and he would look into it. It was a couple of months later when George Thomas was removed from his job and transferred to the Endicott plant. Bob Gridley replaced him. Jack Goetz was removed from his job and transferred to the Burlington, Vermont plant. It was a few months later when I was told to report to Art Cooper's office and I was presented with a FSD Division Award with a check I think for $2500. Later all the division award winners with their wives/husbands were given transportation to Williamsburg, Virginia and treated to a nice weekend of dinners, tours, and entertainment at the older part of the town. Several months later I was notified that the work on Saturn V was reviewed and considered worthy of an IBM Corporate Award which is a very big deal as few are selected and wives/husbands were transported to the Waldorf Astoria in New York City for a weekend of celebration. As I recall this was 1964 or later and I was given a limited edition of a Leonardo Da Vinci with my name imprinted on the cover. I think my son John and his family has the book. In a quite unusual move the next January I received another large check from the corporation that had reviewed the positive financial impact of my work on Saturn V and they had re-evaluated the original award and raised it. What a surprise!

Somewhere along the line and I cannot quite remember the timing I noticed as I continually monitored work on the manufacturing floor of the LA141 machining and processes. I noticed that the fluoride anodizing process had been modified from my patented process to save some time I would guess. I raised the issue and said this was unacceptable and we could not do that as it might not work as good as what we had developed and tested. The lower level managers in manufacturing would not listen so I escalated it to the manufacturing manager George Pisarcheck (sp?) who thought it was not important and would not listen to my urging to go back to the qualified process. So I escalated to the plant manager Art Cooper. This was in the environment of man rated safety and we had posters all over the plant reminding us people's lives depended on our work. Art Cooper called me to his office and when I arrived a smiling George Pisarcheck was there and evidently they had been talking. I don't know about what but I would guess George was trying to poo-poo the young engineer's concerns about doing the process and that it was being done fine. After some civil formalities Art Cooper said that George had told him that the process was being done fine. I did not know what to do, but felt I was so junior that rank would win so I tried something dramatic. I took my IBM badge off and put it on Art's desk and told him George should do the same. We then should take a walk down to the floor and witness the process to see if it was being done the way I had developed it. If it was I would leave IBM for making a mistake. If the process was not being done correctly George should be escorted out of the plant and terminated. At that point George stopped smiling and Art asked him "How about that George?" and George started mumbling and stumbling and Art asked me to leave. George was the plant manager for about another month and then was removed and transferred to the Endicott plant. As you can see in those days IBM rarely terminated people they transferred them and the worse assignment was to a staff position with no work. Most people then found another job outside of IBM and left, although a few reformed and got back in good graces. It was kind of like the penalty box in hockey. The incidents with George Thomas, Jack, and George Pisarcheck led to my reputation as getting managers fired or transferred which was clearly not true. They acted in a way that others saw they should go somewhere else.

R.A. Munroe Earns IBM Award For Outstanding Contribution

Robert A. Munroe of Metallurgical Engineering recently was presented an IBM Outstanding Contribution Award for the introduction of a light weight Lithium-Aluminum Magnesium alloy as a design material in IBM's Saturn V program.

Mr. Munroe worked with Design personnel helping to establish an in-house processing capability including areas of machining, cleaning, handling and finishing.

The citation states, "His outstanding initiative and personal perseverance resulted in usage of Magnesium alloy LA141A as the major structural material in the Saturn V hardware." The major advantage is light weight and stiffness to weight ratio—a high premium requirement. "Our usage represents a major first for IBM and has stimulated high interest at NASA as a design material."

R. Munroe Gets Supplemental Award for Major Contribution

Robert A. Munroe of Metallurgical Engineering has been presented a supplemental award to an IBM Outstanding Contribution Award which was presented to him recently. (Announced in January 20, 1966 IBM News.)

His award was for the introduction of a stronger, light-weight Lithium-Aluminum Magnesium alloy as a design material for hardware being used in IBM's Saturn IB/V program. Mr. Munroe worked with Design personnel helping to establish in-house processing capability including areas of machining, cleaning, handling and finishing.

His citation states, "His outstanding initiative and personal perseverance resulted in usage of Magnesium alloy LA141A as the major structural material in the Saturn V hardware." The major advantage is light weight, and stiffness to weight ratio—a high premium requirement. "Our usage represents a major first for IBM and has stimulated high interest at NASA as a design material."

The supplemental award illustrates the importance of his outstanding contribution, and recognizes the wide value, its potential use of his idea, which solves a serious corrosion problem inherent in lithium-aluminum magnesium alloys.

NASA has recognized the process as having a broad importance and application to NASA, the military and other industries and is recommending its use be instituted in numerous areas of development.

Robert A. Munroe of Metallurgical Engineering is shown with a Launch Vehicle Digital Computer (LVDC) frame, cut up in order to set quality standards for the Saturn IB computer. The frame is made of the Lithium-Aluminum Magnesium LA141A alloy for which Mr. Munroe received his contribution award.

Robert A. Munroe, center, discusses his Outstanding Contribution Award with, left to right, John A. Goetz, manager of Component and Materials Engineering; General Manager John B. Jackson who presented the award; William F. Schweizer Jr., manager of Special Engineering; and Robert J. Gridley, manager of Metallurgical Engineering.

Promoted

Robert A. Munroe
Staff Engineer
Metallurgical
Eng'g (581)

G. W. Carter   R. A. Munroe

Carter, Munroe Papers Voted 'Best of Session'

Seven IBM authors, four of them from the Space Guidance Center, presented technical papers at the National Electronic Packaging and Production Conference in Long Beach, Calif., in June. Of the SGC four, two were selected as "Best of the Session."

Papers and authors from the SGC were:

"Thermal Design of the Saturn V Launch Vehicle Digital Computer and Data Adapter" by Michael J. Donegan and Bruno R. Pagnani;

"A State-of-the-Art Evaluation of Infrared in Heat Transfer Engineering" by Glenn W. Carter;

"The Use of Magnesium Alloys in Aerospace Electronic Packaging" by Robert A. Munroe; and "Automatic Saturn V Page Test System by Walter Wylie.

Twelve papers, one from each session, were selected by the audience at the conference as "Best of Session." Two of the Owego papers, Mr. Carter's and Mr. Munroe's, were selected, and the authors were awarded $50 and wallplaque certificates. The 12 papers will be published by Electronic Packaging and Production in the July to September issues. The readers will then select from these 12 the paper adjudged by them to be the "Best of the Conference." The author of this paper will receive an additional $200.

Twenty-Two SGC Inventors Honored

Twenty-two Space Guidance Center engineering personnel recently were honored at an inventors' luncheon for patent applications filed or for patent disclosures published. The inventors and those participating in the program are, left to right: front, Lawrence Cooper, Richard W. Kern, Russell D. Shoultes, John J. Walsh, manager of the SGC Engineering Laboratory; General Manager Arthur E. Cooper, Warner E. Stillings and G. Alf Malmros of Patent Engineering; and Roger S. Smith, manager of Patent Operations; second row, Harley A. Cloud, James W. Dieffenderfer, Louis E. Peterson, Charles V. McNeil, Frederic C. Fitzgerald, William E. Goetz, Thomas Nielsen and Albert W. Vinal; and back row, Ralph J. Riley, Robert A. Tuttle, James J. Kiernan, Robert A. Watson, Aldon D. Berard and Robert A. Munroe. Absent when the picture was taken were Robert Betts, Samuel R. Pulford and Lawrence R. Yetter.

And a story often told about me is true, but I have to set the context. On many of the FDS programs the main cast of characters often worked many long hours at the plant and 6 day weeks were not unusual. I became at least a junior member of the main cast and on every new program or crisis I could name in advance the programmers, the circuit designers, the electronic packaging people, the materials people, and manufacturing engineers in advance. Sounds like a big cast but it usually was one person from each area. Sometimes in extremes we would seek out a first aid room (usually one to a building) and take a nap at night which made the nurses mad because we were taking rest breaks on their clean beds. The cold war days were intense and FSD had important parts to play in that and the race to the moon. Some people drank too much. Some families broke up, although a lot of the wives helped each other and with the children. And in some cases you got slap happy from the lack of sleep. So one night when the guards were putting up the posters for the next week I did it. The posters were all over the halls of each of the 5 buildings (multiple floors) and were reminding us of safety or quality or something like that. Well this one weekend night they were putting up posters with 2 silhouettes horizontal showing heads coming together and the poster said in giant letters, DO YOU KNOW HOW TO GIVE MOUTH TO MOUTH RESUSCITATION?". So I went around at a discreet distance from the guards and inked in giant letters, WITHOUT GETTING EMOTIONALLY INVOLVED?".

By Monday lunch time all the posters were down. I don't think they ever knew who did it or I would have been in big trouble. I would have pleaded temporary insanity which was true.

I would be amiss if I did not mention a backup plan to make the LVDC a different way from drilling holes for the cooling liquid. A backup effort led by Bob Skelding was undertaken in case Brooks and Perkins was not successful in casting billets with defects so small they woud not cause leaks after machining. Bob worked with Wellman Bronze in Bay City, Michigan to cast the LA141 material around small stainless steel tubes bent into a serpentine shape to replace the drilled holes in the walls of the LVDC. After a few tries one or more billets were cast which upon X-Ray examination showed the tubes in the correct position and a billet was started in the computer controlled machining process when the word was given to Bob that the effort should be stopped. As I understand it NASA wanted the holes drilled in the walls after the cast billets improved in quality so that no weld repairs would be needed (this was after billet #35). The backup effort led by Bob Skelding was an elegant solution and was as important as learning how to drill the long cooling holes accurately and I think was not used to keep on a tight schedule driven by launching men to the moon before the end of the decade which was President John Kennedy's goal.

Poscript:

I found out later from Martin (Marty) Cardwell that the IU was seeing a lot of hours with coolant in it during tests at Cape Kennedy, and he had been called in as the LA141 alloy used in the LVDC was reacting with the coolant and causing a lot of hydrogen to be produced, which in turn caused high pressures in the cooling system and corrosion caused by the LA141 corroding the aluminum cold plates. When I advised using the LA141 I was told there would not be extensive hours with coolant in the lines of the LVDC and LVDA. Marty came up with a solution which was to pump "water glass" a mixture of sodium and potassium silicate (used to coat eggs to extend life) through the LVDC and LVDA and that coating cut the corrosion significantly and solved the problem of alkalinity and high pressure. A very clever solution by Marty.

Chapter 6
We Didn't Do That

In the last month of the Lyndon B. Johnson administration (1963-1969) his Attorney General of the United States Ramsey Clark had the Department of Justice file an anti-trust suit against IBM. The thinking was that IBM had too much of the computer business. This suit lasted 13 years and in the end was dropped. Along the timeline the computer business was rapidly transforming to more power in smaller computers and there were more competitors which was the argument IBM lawyers had made all the time. No matter, during the duration of the suit we were strictly forbidden to make contact or cooperate with the competitors in the computer business. There was an exception and that was for national security and IBM worked with the U.S. Navy I know to provide disk drives for submarines (IBM San Jose drives hardened for military use) where the processors were provided by someone else. The integration of the hardware required close cooperation so that was allowed.

However, early in the Saturn V program NASA approached IBM asking for help to make the RCA computers at Cape Kennedy more reliable. The DOJ had not filed the anti-trust suit yet (1969) but had filed anti-trust suits against IBM starting in 1956 (consent decree) which forbid IBM to just lease computers and when they sold them they had to sell the new owners parts. IBM used to provide most of the punched cards in the country (millions per day) with a unique press called the Carroll Press after its IBM inventor. IBM had to sell those to others and eventually got out of the printing business for punched cards. So that was the environment when NASA asked IBM to help RCA make their computers more reliable as they would not run for 24 hours continuously (which NASA wanted) at the Cape. During the build up of the manned space program there was a lot of pressure by companies and their congressional representatives to use other computers besides IBM that NASA favored because of their reliability and service.

IBM was in a quandary as working with RCA would get it in trouble with the DOJ and not working with RCA would get it in trouble with NASA with its mandate to the moon by the end of the decade given by President Kennedy. So a small team at FSD Owego was put together and sworn to secrecy to help RCA. There were the MLB designers and manufacturing engineering people, solder experts in the materials laboratory, and very few others. Materials laboratory people analyzed the RCA failed boards (no shortage of them) and found at least 2 significant problems. One was the plated through holes to make connections from one layer to another were very poor in quality and the solder joints of the components (leads through some of the holes) were not designed properly. IBMers met with RCA engineers and chemists and told them what they had to do to change to make their MLBs more reliable and took them through the IBM plant and showed them equipment, quality controls, and every detail of the IBM Owego advanced processes. A year or two earlier IBM Owego had to teach the board makers at IBM Endicott the same thing when they started making MLBs. The RCA engineers also were told how to make their solder joints reliable and during this time several trips were made by some Owego engineers to the RCA plant where they made their MLBs and reviewed processes there and made recommended changes. RCA changed the way they made there MLBs and solder joints and got new boards to the NASA computers on a priority basis and the reliability improved markedly as you would expect. All the IBM Owego team members that helped RCA were then instructed to turn in all notebooks, notes, and records and they were destroyed by IBM Security personnel. We had our own security guards and they carried guns until one shot out a clock playing with his firearm on a boring night. So we were forbidden by the Department of Justice (DOJ) to help RCA (we never asked because we knew), but we did and NASA knew and it really happened but their is no proof.

During the Saturn V program when IBM was designing and building the LVDC and LVDA NASA came to IBM and told them you have to make the Saturn Switch Selector (SSS) because the original supplier could not build them and pass the brutal tests (some of the SSS units were mounted near the Stage I engines with horrendous vibration). IBM did not think this was a wonderful offer because the SSS units were mostly relays and were not mainly processors. NASA basically made them an offer they could not refuse ("Do you want future work? If so, make the SSS.". So we made the SSS and made them well and they worked. So NASA management from the top down would look to IBM to make things well and make them work from the commercial type computers on the ground doing calculations to OAO, Gemini, and now Saturn V project. Making the SSS was not a secret, how we got the job was.

This successful record led to another project which was doing a backup of the MIT Draper Laboratory and Raytheon Lunar Landing Module computer. The MIT Draper Laboratory was famous for the development of radar and inertial guidance. MIT was to do the design and Raytheon was to build it and they were way behind schedule and NASA was worried. So NASA asked IBM FSD Owego to design a backup. Again, this was a sensitive project and I don't believe MIT or Raytheon knew. We did a design on paper for electrical equivalence and a mechanical design that would fit in the same space. No hardware was made as MIT and Raytheon came through at the last minute and we were told to destroy all records. This was done possibly to avoid any appearance of anti-trust by outdoing Raytheon who at that time had made some computers although they were not used outside of the DOD except the short lived 5 parallel processor Liberator computer built around 1959. The Liberator was a brilliant concept at the time but no one could really program it easily.

Christopher Kraft of NASA was very demanding in services and equipment which was important to get people safely on rockets and send them into space and have them return safely and he drove contractors mercilessly. After the successful landing on the moon and more missions some of the intensity seemed to die down with the contractors in his eyes. It is said he called the president of IBM and told him that IBM FSD was not doing a good job or words to that effect. You can imagine that started an investigation and lots of executives at corporate headquarters and FSD headquarters was very involved. After much work and long hours the president of

IBM got back with Christopher Kraft and said he had looked into it and IBM was doing everything in the contract. Kraft's response was basically "You don't get it. The reason we favored IBM was you always went above and beyond the minimum requirements.". IBM and most US businesses did not understand that to be successful you should go beyond expectations. Something that became more meaningful as companies started to lose business years later to Japanese and German manufacturers and a few new US companies.

I did some work on the Manned Orbiting Laboratory (MOL) and spent 6 months in Thousand Oaks, California which allegedly was going to be a permanent facility. The family moved there about June 1969 and I elected to go to IBM FSD in Huntsville, Alabama after being told I had to move somewhere in November 1969. I interviewed in Burlington, Vermont and Poughkeepsie, New York and decided I did not want to be part of a huge group that seldom could see the fruits of their labor and were so bureaucratic it was hard to get things done. The MOL was advertised to be an orbiting science laboratory but was a thinly disguised spy lab in the sky and the Russians knew it. The program was killed in late 1969 and the DOD recession hit hard. I can remember aerospace companies in southern California laying off thousands of people per week with hardly any notice. There was short period where I was "rented" out to an aerospace company (North American) in Seal Beach, California and had to drive from Thousand Oaks every day and we were to report to the facility at 8 am and not leave until 5 pm. Of course since the few of us who were "rented" out were engineers we got paid for gas at government rates but did not get any money for the time spent traveling.

The work at North American was seeing if we could figure out how to connect many flip chips with aluminum bumps that were ultrasonically attached to MLBs. I am not sure why North American chose this course instead of solder bumps which IBM had openly published all the details of how to do it in technology papers. North American would have not been under patent regulations for DOD work like this. The satellite they were trying to build was the KH-1 I believe. We could not help them with their chosen technology which would cause defects in their chips and we could not convince them to use solder bump technology so we parted ways. It was the second look I had at a small piece of the intelligence world which had started when I saw a U2 wing mockup at Sanders Associates about 1957.

When my work on LA141 first got published on the Saturn V project (couple of magazines) I was contacted by a metallurgist from Lockheed and I think his name was Elliott Willner. He wanted me to go to California and talk about a project he was working on. When I flew there and followed the directions I ended up at the Lockheed "Skunk Works". The security was the tightest in real terms that I ever experienced even in areas called Secret. Once inside a lot of the equipment or structures were covered in sheets. I was led to an Agena D satellite and the question was if I thought LA141 could be used to house the camera. I heard all the requirements and my opinion that it didn't appear to be a good application. Even though LA141 had a stiffness to weight ratio that was very high I thought the high thermal expansion would be a negative hard to overcome with the temperature excursions anticipated. We had some detailed discussions outside of the large manufacturing floor about the application and general applications where I thought the material may be useful. I was thanked and led to where my rental car was located. I don't know if Lockheed ever used the material or not.

I wrote a technical paper on LA141 and its application on Gemini and Saturn V which was going to be presented at an electronics packaging conference in Montreal, Canada. Before I traveled I was at work and was called to go see Security in the main building at IBM Owego. There was a man with no ID badge sitting at a desk and he never identified himself which was a clue. He told me it was likely I would be approached by some people from the Metals Science Agency in Russia and I was to be careful that I revealed only what I had put in my paper and several magazine articles. I said I understood and agreed and I left. Remember this was the Cold War period between the US and Russia. At the conference I was approached by some Russian "scientists" and after a general discussion they asked about ballistic impact properties and I said truthfully that I did not know anything in that area as I had only worked on electronic packaging applications for space structures. That was the end of it. Later in the year I found out that the Franklin

Arsenal of the US Army was investigating LA141 and variants to absorb shrapnel after going through armor plate. I don't think they ever used it, but I know an aluminum honeycomb structure has been used on some of our lightweight armored vehicles.

People today think of all the data that the intelligence agencies have at their disposal, but they are probably unaware of the huge databases that existed over 40 years ago. IBM at San Jose, California under contract to the Central Intelligence Agency (CIA) made a complex write once, read data storage unit that wrote on glass slides that had great resolution film on them. Data could be written by an electronic beam which was much better than any light source including even today's lasers. The glass slides were about the size of a box of cigarettes (long kind) that you see in stores. The plastic boxes would hold multiple slides and after data was written on a slide and an index number it was developed with wet chemistry (the Achilles heal of the machine) and put in a box. There were hundreds of these boxes in the machine which could be accessed and then read into large computers so users could access the data. I don't know the capacity of the machine I saw in a laboratory, but it was many terabytes. Someone in the US Air Force I believe or perhaps the CIA wanted IBM FSD Owego to see if we could compact this machine which was in a room of about 500 square feet and make it so it would fit in a satellite. Remember we could launch tons at that time, but only in the largest rockets which normally would not be used for a satellite at that time. The wet chemistry storage and control was very maintenance intensive on the ground and the electron beam unit was large even without the vacuum system (not needed in space). Perhaps we were not imaginative enough, but we thought there was a better way than that. The project was called Walnut (a hard nut to crack and it was. For several years pictures were taken by high resolution cameras in satellites and film canisters ejected and at a low altitude a parachute would come out and an airplane with a tail hook would snare the parachute and haul it in so the film could be analyzed when the plane landed. Tricky to pull off and took a lot of skill but most of the missions were very successful.

When our youngest son David who was visually impaired got in middle school it was about 1982 and we had an early version of an IBM Personal Computer (PC). When it came time to do library research he could not use the school library so I signed up with a service run out of Palo Alto, California which was originally started by a government agency. Non-classified documents and books could be accessed digitally (we had dial up phone internet) at our house. A business with an expensive monthly subscription could access documents and technical reports at any time. We had a very low cost monthly subscription which allowed users to access books, documents, and reports "after normal business hours". David used that even though it was awkward it allowed him to be independent as we had a laboratory version of software and equipment that would allow the visually impaired to have the computer "speak" and he could print out the information and use a Kurzweill scanner at the school to change it to Braille if needed. I found that every American Chemical Society (ACS) journal ever printed back to the late 19th century was in that database as well as many journals and documents in Russian, German, and Japanese. One could only guess what agency would want a database like that.

Chapter 7
4Pi Computers

After Saturn V was well under way and in parallel with much work a series of computer designs started at IBM FSD Owego called 4Pi. The commercial computers and accessories were called System 360 and were the first operating system computers where applications could be written. In geometry 360 is the number of degrees of a circle (2 Pi). 4Pi in steridians represents a sphere or a 3 dimensional System 360. The FSD Owego computers were designed to be compatible with the commercial computers from a software view and simulations could be performed on the commercial computers. Up to this time every computer in the government DOD had different word lengths and operating systems which resulted in too much complexity and expense.

The basic building block of the 4Pi computers would be similar to the Saturn V pages. For a good overall view of the technical details of the series of 4Pi computer system model TC (tactical processor) for low end applications), model CP (customized processor) for intermediate applications, and EP (extended performance) for large-scale processing see the following:

http://bitsavers.trailing-edge.com/pdf/ibm/4pi Technical_Description_of_IBM_System_4_Pi_Computers_1967.pdf

This is a picture taken from the reference above showing two connectors on the wide page which is simply two wide Saturn V page using the reliable high density connector IBM had developed for the Saturn V program.

A big difference in the circuits for the 4Pi programs were integrated circuits in hermetically sealed metal flatpacks that utilized surface mount technology which IBM had pioneered on the Saturn V program. Texas Instruments had pioneered the integrated circuits, but IBM did not use anyone's integrated circuits for the Saturn V program or System 360 computers because they cost more and were not as reliable as the IBM components. This was challenged even in IBM but AT&T did a review at IBM request and were surprised that at the time (1964) IBM committed their components like ULDs to Saturn V and SLTs to System 360 the IBM components were far more reliable and lower cost than AT&T had estimated in the early 1960s.

However, by 1967 the integrated circuits had become lower cost and more reliable although problems occurred frequently which IBM addressed by special quality controls. The multi-layer printed circuit boards (MLBs) were pioneered on Gemini and used on Saturn V. Some literature references call them multilayer interconnection boards or MIBs but they are the same thing. As more and more circuits could be put on the silicon chips and they got faster the computers were continually changed to increase performance at a high rate.

IBM 4Pi computers were used on various DOD aircraft like the F-111 (2 computers), the E6, E3, F-15, B-52, and the A6. NASA applications were Skylab, MOL (Manned Orbiting Laboratory), and Shuttle. The shuttle used 5 AP-101S computers and were the first to synchronize both software and hardware. 4 computers were originally planned to do all the work and the 5th would be a backup to take over if one of the 4 failed. With time as more and more demands were put on the computers and they were found to be very reliable the 5th was brought on board full time. A good reference for 4Pi on space applications can be found at:

http://www.hq.nasa.gov/office/pao/History/computers/Ch3-3.html

The MOL did not have the stringent weight requirements of the Saturn V computer and circuit technology had advanced quickly which allowed much more computing capability than the Saturn V vintage electronics. The decision was made by the box designers to use AZ31B magnesium for most of the structure and to make an extruded aluminum shape with a hole in the center to mount to the top of the magnesium box shape to provide the liquid cooling path. The extruded aluminum shape could easily be cut and welded to provide a continuous path to mount the new double width pages to. Thus the integrally cooled MOL computer took the idea from the Saturn V and updated it. Not as light as the LA141, but less expensive and light enough and did not require the special handling and corrosion protection that the Saturn V computer did.

The 4Pi computers for aircraft were packaged in aluminum structures that used air cooling provided by the compressor stage of the jet engines during flight. The challenge there was the requirement to have no cooling for several minutes when the compressor cooling was shut off to provide maximum thrust to the plane for take off. This was a real challenge in Vietnam with its regular high temperatures on the runway. I had very little involvement with the 4Pi computer packaging or manufacturing, but they were very significant production programs for IBM FSD Owego.

The US Navy had invested a large amount of money for combined environmental testing of the hardware for its E6 program. The traditional tests were to run thermal cycling, vibrations, shock, and other tests serially. The chambers for the E6 program were very expensive and did vibration and temperature cycling while being electrically tested. The theory was that this would produce a more reliable box by finding manufacturing defects if any. In reality the program did not. The best indicator of a faulty circuit line in a board or a faulty solder joint was to vibrate the assembly and then electrically test. This later was adopted for IBM PCs and I saw the same thing done with VCR tape decks in Japan. A low cost test and very efficient in finding defects.

By the time the shuttle was being designed and the AP-101S computers being designed in FSD Owego I was in Huntsville, Alabama at IBM and the manager of a hybrid circuit laboratory. We did development of multi-layer thick film ceramic modules, special high performance circuits, and special circuits that allegedly could not be built by others in the industry. At one point we were asked to build some special circuits NOT to be used on the shuttle (we were not NASA man rated certified). These special circuits were to be used to check out the shuttle electronics because the supplier building the production parts was way behind schedule. I was very concerned that the modules we were building would be used for test and possibly find their way into flight equipment as I am skeptical of controls of equipment. I was aware that non-certified parts painted international orange were found in a Titan ballistic missile computer at Cape Kennedy which were working fine, but found when a technician on the launch pad took the covers off the computer to replace a faulty part (not the non-certified) and found the orange painted modules. International orange is that bright orange you see on Coast Guard ships and aircraft because of its high visibility.

The Titan story was told to me by Hugh McNeill who was an Air Force officer and told me this happened at Cape Kennedy. The computer was in a Titan missile to undergo a test launch with production hardware. The computer had some kind of problem (eventually found not to be in the international painted unqualified modules) and had to be removed while the missile was on the launch pad. To delay a launch while many ships and aircraft were at sea in the launch window cost many millions of dollars a day and no one wanted to be responsible for a launch delay. So when the command center queried all the facilities involved Hugh's experienced commander declared the missile was ready to go. Hugh was amazed because the computer was removed on the gantry, covers off it, and they were waiting for a replacement! Hugh's commander knew others might very well not be ready so he was playing a game of chicken. Sure enough as the command center continued their querying a distant radar site said they were not and it would cause a delay. This gave Hugh and his commander sufficient time to get a replacement computer, have the technicians install it, put the cover on the missile where the computer was located and checked it out. The Cape was not responsible for the delay.

We made the special circuit modules in Huntsville and painted them the bright international orange and marked them as non-flight as well as the part number. We built the modules for test about 1977. After the Challenger disaster in 1986 NASA and all the contractors investigated all the hardware on the ground to make sure all of it was flight ready and of the correct quality. By 1986 I was in Austin, Texas at IBM after a 4 year stay at IBM in Boulder, Colorado. I was called while in Austin, Texas, again managing a special hybrid circuit laboratory, and asked if I remember building some special modules for the space shuttle. Yes I did remember that. Well an examination of some IBM flight hardware had found some bright orange modules made at IBM Huntsville. The caller urgently asked "They were flight qualified, right?" and I answered no that is why they are painted international orange. He tried to get me to say they were flight certified and I refused to go along. The modules were evidently put in for test and worked fine for years and no one noticed and they may very well have worked fine in flight, but I was not going to say we were certified for that part when we were not. Amazing that bright orange parts in 2 instances that I am aware of did not raise attention when in equipment as long as it was working fine. That is scary!

Chapter 8
Hybrid Circuits

After the brief stay in California and I had chosen Huntsville, Alabama I was asked to start a hybrid circuit laboratory using thick film technology. This was about 1970 and the technology was basically the same as used in the IBM FSD ULDs in the Saturn V LVDC and LVDA and the IBM Components Division SLTs used in commercial computers starting with the System 360 computers. As a refresher this meant in the FSD case using a pattern of holes in a very high mesh stainless steel screen and then firing the conductive or resistive inks about 850°C in a continuously moving mesh belt oven. Making artwork on T-shirts or other materials is very similar but nowhere as precise. In the FSD case a squeegee pushed the ink across the screen to deposit the ink on a small ceramic substrate which usually was alumina (aluminum oxide) or in some high power cases it was beryllia (beryllium oxide).

Ed Massey was instrumental in helping me start the laboratory and Bruno Pagnani lobbied to have me made manager for which I will always feel he did me wrong as a friend, but was good for me in many ways. We reported to an engineer manager who was so hard working it was unbelievable and integrity beyond description and that was Ken Harris. Last I knew he retired in Huntsville. Ed retired to Arab just south of Huntsville. Jim Honeycutt a metallurgist was brought on board to learn about wire bonding, Bill Clayton (eccentric genius in his way) was made responsible for learning about thick film materials and screening. Tom Battle was a technician who happened to be black and was a product of an IBM FSD training program to upgrade locally hired talent. He was very smart, patient, and very skilled. In today's world he might be a manufacturing manager. Earl McPeters was another technician that went through the same program and was steady but not as talented as Tom Battle. A third technician was Andrew Bahl and I think he went through the IBM FSD training program, but I am not sure.

Bob Christiansen who I knew from FSD Owego handled the organic materials side and is an absolutely whiz on applications and materials. He is retired in Salvisa, Kentucky west of Lexington. Bill Clayton was in charge of the abrasive trimmer set up and programming and later a laser trimmer. We had some manufacturing technicians transferred to us from the regular manufacturing floor. There was Kathy (later married Bob Christiansen), Harold Tibbs (outstanding in productivity and quality in wire bonding), and Peggy Clark who came off a farm in Tennessee and was good mechanically and eventually was sent to school with Tom Battle where the Hughes programmable wire bonders were made so she could do set up and repair. Remember this was at the time that women were supposed to do the mundane and sometimes boring job of wire bonding and not be a machine technician but she was good and that was my decision. The decision much to some of the manufacturing management chagrin as they were stuck in the mode of what was "women's work".

I worked with the lead people in the department and we designed an area that had a small modest clean room, a laser and air-abrasive trimming area, a firing area with three belt ovens (started out with one), and a small room for measurements. Small offices near the total area were for the engineers. Starting out small the department eventually grew to about 15 people total and included some physical design layout engineers. Ron Crawford was one of the physical layout engineers and after he retired from IBM he lived in southern Florida, but I lost track of him.

Ed Massey led the electrical design group and some of the design engineers I recall were Gus Schrottke, Denny Oliver, and Chip Conklin. Chip Conklin was a bright engineer who left us after a couple of years and went to Hughes Electronics in southern California and became a director the last I heard. Ed was a components engineer at NASA before he joined IBM in Huntsville and had a broad background which really helped us in the thick film laboratory as we learned how to handle un-packaged semi-conductors. We would buy un-packaged semi-conductors from integrated circuits (ICs) to power chips. The manager over Ed Massey and me was Hugh McNeill who had an electrical background and when in the US Air Force worked on one of the first ballistic missile sites in North Dakota. He had some interesting stories to tell about the early days of testing (at Cape Kennedy) and getting the missile sites operational. He died in December, 2014 in the Raleigh, North Carolina area.

Between Ed and I we had about 30 people involved at the height of operation and we could make any device with thick film technology up to 4 inches by 4 inches and 1/8 inch thick. Most of the parts were smaller and probably averaged 1 inch by 1 inch and 1/16 inch thick. We did ICs by wire bond or flip chip solder bump interconnect and the wire bonding varied from 0.0007 inch diameter gold or aluminum up to 0.015 inch diameter aluminum. The gold wire maximum diameter we could handle was 0.005 inch diameter. The human hair varies from about 0.0025 inches to 0.004 inches in diameter to give you a reference.

Most of the substrates were single sided but we did some high frequency parts that we drilled holes in with the laser (or had them specially molded if they were a production part. By using special screening techniques and a holder for the substrate with a vacuum we could get the conductor paste into the hole and connect the front and back sides. On one project we screened multiple layers of conductor and insulator pastes and made multi-layer thick film substrates which was fairly advanced in the early 1970s because the conductors were about 0.004 inches wide and we had voltage and ground planes that were almost solid (in area). The combination of almost solid and thin conductors with connections between conductor layers caused large differences in shrinkage and cracking could occur. Maintaining integrity of each individual layer was very difficult and Bill Clayton was very innovative and persistent in developing the art of screening for these parts. The alumina and beryllia substrates usually came from the ceramics division of 3M (they supplied the parts for IBM Components Division) and from Coors Ceramics (yes, a division of the beer company).

It is important to note that production for us was a very low number overall. Our specialty was to make circuits that were reliable and unique in that most people in the industry thought the parts could not be made at all. We also worked with some of the most advanced ICs at the time and learning how to work with CMOS (complimentary metal oxide semiconductor) technology which was very sensitive to static electricity was new to us and many others.

One of the production parts we made was for the Application Technology Satellite (ATS) that was designed to transmit from space to the ground a signal strong enough that a simple receiver could work with the signal. At the time large satellite dishes (several feet in diameter) were needed to receive signals from satellites as the signals were very weak. Later in the 20th century satellites were launched that sent much stronger signals allowing home to have small receiver dishes as used with TVs Dish Network and Direct TV. One of the uses of the ATS was to allow doctors in remote areas to transmit to the satellite using portable ground equipment (not very small) and to receive back information. That way a doctor in a remote area could transmit vital information to a medical center hundreds or thousands of miles away and let experts help him/her diagnose a patient problem and suggest solutions. This application was tested successfully in western Colorado. Another use was to transmit educational programs to remote villages in India with no schools or electricity. The ground receiver would work from batteries charged by solar power and the receiver could be a simple as a metal frame umbrella and the receiver module would be clamped to the umbrella handle and slid up and down to get the most optimum signal. The umbrella had to be pointed roughly to the part of the sky where the village was told ahead of time, but with the strong signal it did not have to be super accurate. My understanding is that the educational program with ATS in India was successfully demonstrated. A picture of a module with the hybrid circuits built in our laboratory is shown below. The small covers were molded alumina and adhesive bonded with a special epoxy resin and method largely developed by Bob Christiansen and this made a hermetic seal which was unknown at the time with an organic resin. The process required a vacuum chamber while curing. NASA certified this even for man-rated space use and we were the first facility to get this certification which also included metal filled epoxy resin joining of chip passive components like resistors and capacitors. In order to be man-rated the part basically had to pass severe environmental and life testing. In the 1970s most metal filled resin adhesives lost conductivity over time and the challenge was not to have degradation.

ATS Marks First Space Use of Huntsville-Built Hybrids

A PAGE WORTH NOTING...is this page destined for use aboard the first Applications Technology Satellite (ATS) prototype. The page represents a milestone for ATS activity at ESC/Huntsville. It marks the first ATS page to be populated with ESC/Huntsville-built hybrid circuit modules. It also marks another first — the first space use of the locally manufactured modules.

Unlike OAO, the Applications Technology Satellite hasn't flown yet, and won't until mid-1973. However, a significant milestone in IBM's ATS activity was passed in mid-November when the first ESC/Huntsville-built hybrid modules were populated or mounted on a page slated for the first ATS prototype.

The occasion was a dual milestone. It marked the first use of hybrids in IBM-built ATS hardware, and their use marks the first space use of the locally built hybrid modules. Four ESC/Huntsville departments were involved in the ATS milestone. Hybrid Packaging Technology (298), managed by Robert A. Munroe, built the modules. Prototype Manufacturing and Processing Labs (197), managed by George D. Case, created the circuit boards. Model Shop and Fabrication (194), managed by Hubert C. Shawn, created the special forming tool to cut and crimp the module leads. Circuit Board Population (198), managed by Russ K. Rose, populated the boards.

As a subcontractor to Fairchild Industries, IBM is responsible for design and development of the telemetry and command subsystem for ATS. The command portion of the subsystem allows a ground station controller to control satellite operations such as turning equipment on and off or to direct the satellite to execute certain maneuvers. The telemetry portion provides a radio link between the satellite and ground stations to relay status and condition of onboard equipment and experiments. Also aboard ATS will be an IBM-developed and built interferometer which will precisely measure the direction of signals transmitted from ground stations on earth to determine the satellite's exact attitude.

IBM/FSD activity on ATS is divided between ESC/Huntsville and FSC/Gaithersburg.

What is not obvious in the photo is that the materials used were a relatively complex system since the conductors were wire bonded to gold circuit lines, but the copper clips were soldered on to the substrate and circuit board was a gold-palladium mix which allowed solderability with lead tin solders and was compatible with the gold circuit lines. The screened on conductors made "bumps" about 0.001 inches high so the gaps had to be filled with an insulator to provide a more flat area for the epoxy seal. Also, note that individual parts are serialized and records were kept on individual parts so if there were problems in the future all process steps could be reviewed. This was typical of NASA practice and for early DOD parts. Today most military and NASA parts are off the shelf commercial parts that may or may not be specially tested for electrical characteristics over a wider range of temperatures. The parts not meeting the test requirements for the wider temperature range would be sold on the commercial market. Also, the lead design for the package combined with the knowledge of the optimum thickness solder joints between the leads and substrate and between the leads and the printed circuit board were known from the extensive experience on the Saturn V ULDs and the follow up 4Pi products using the TI flatpacks.

A very demanding part to make was a 10 stage log-IF amplifier (a very high frequency radar part) made for the secret (then) Wild Weasel program that enabled aircraft to detect the exact location of an enemy radar. Early radar detection equipment for aircraft involved having an receiver on each wing tip and one in the nose and by comparing when the signal arrived (using an accurate clock) it would do a triangulation calculation and give a location to a weapons operator. The Wild Weasel system shrunk this to about a 6 inch diameter which required a very accurate clock and very fast and accurate circuits. A 6 inch diameter receiver would allow the system to be put in a missile which would could be launched to destroy the enemy radar instead of an operator finding the radar and launching a "blind" missile which was not as accurate as desired. The 10 stage log-IF amplifier was a substrate about 4 inches long by 1 inch wide and 1/16 thick as I recall. At least 10 holes were in the substrate so connections could be made from the circuitry on the top to the solid conductor ground plane on the back. Microwave transistors (very fast and touchy) were used and the length of the gold wire bonds kept as constant as possible (they acted like inductors). We tuned the capacitance of each stage by using a laser to carefully trim or remove metal from around where the chip was wire bonded. This type of work was typical of the coordination of Ed's circuit experts and the people in the hybrid laboratory. Using a method similar to that I described for the ATS modules when a part met all the stringent requirements a molded alumina cap would be bonded and the part serialized. They were sent to IBM FSD Owego to be assembled on to circuit boards and made part of module for the total system. I believe that some of the first systems we shipped were sent to the Israeli's and used in their fighters in the Yom Kippur war in 1973.

Somewhere in my 7 year stay at Huntsville the need came up to determine how much current a wire bond could carry and remain reliable. The industry method was to force current through the wire and when it melted (fusing current) back off some which was similar to derating a capacitor which was familiar to electrical designers. This seemed archaic to me and not very good from an engineering view as wires slowly pulsed would heat and cool and could fatigue and wire bond fatigue failures were not unknown on the wires carrying the power source for the semiconductor device. I went back to my heat transfer studies in graduate school and found a 19th century solution which was used to measure thermal conductivity of metals by forcing current through a rod. Later this formula was used to design filaments in light bulbs. About the 1930s Langmuir of GE updated it for radiation for high temperature filaments. I ignored radiation as it would be small component of the conduction term. For simplicity I assumed that half the heat in the wire would be transmitted to the substrate and half to the semiconductor surface. In reality since the semiconductor would dissipate heat that end of the wire was unlikely to sink as much heat as the substrate, but the assumption was an even split. Based on those assumptions the wire would reach its highest temperature in the center. A rise of $25C^o$ was assumed as a very reliable wire bond and a rise of $50C^o$ was assumed to be reliable for consumer products. Using these assumptions I made an Excel[c] spreadsheet where the constants for aluminum wire and gold wire were put in and the user could choose the maximum temperature rise desired, the type of wire, and the length. The length could be estimated from the preliminary layout of the part. The answer would be what diameter wire should be used for direct current. If the answer was less than 0.0007 inch diameter for gold or 0.001 inch diameter for aluminum then use that minimum wire which was based on manufacturing limits. If the number came out higher round up to the next nearest standard diameter which ran in increments of 0.001 inches. I also ran a root mean square formula where the designer could put in the frequency and the designer would get an estimate of how much more current could be carried at that frequency. It had an upper limit in frequency which was determined by the maximum rise in temperature. Think of it this way; if the frequency is 100 times a second and the pulse is very narrow then the wire is carrying no current for most of the second so has a chance to dissipate the heat for that period. Trust me it worked. Later Dr. Ronald Tomeck worked out an exact solution which only varied at the very high frequencies from my estimate. Later (about 1985) I came across a PhD paper given at an IEEE conference where the author solved the problem another way. No one bothered to do a literature search and see the equation developed about 1890.

Another estimating tool I developed based on empirical experience was to take the area of the component and multiply by a factor (determined by experience) and when all the numbers were added up you would have a fair estimate of the minimum substrate size required. Prior to this every design was laid out by the physical designers and might have to be redone several times to get the minimum size. The estimator I developed usually cut the layout design to one time therefore being more efficient. It also allowed others to put multiple virtual substrates on a PCB or another substrate and know what the larger assembly would require in area.

A very unique project was to replace the IBM analog bombing computer on the B-52 with a digital unit that could be programmed to drop as many as 200 bombs in an offset pattern so that overlapping damage would occur on the ground. This was for use in Vietnam to destroy tunnel systems underneath the jungle canopy. A squadron of B-52s with 500 pound bombs could fly in formation and reportedly destroy the ground underneath it with overlapping craters for nearly a mile wide and several miles long. The digital computer would fly the planes once over the target area. The digital unit was to fit in the same space as the small analog computer which could only control a few bombs and it had to be programmed with thumb wheels which was difficult with gloves worn for the high altitudes flown. There were several modules made in the hybrid circuit laboratory that were very special.

One module consisted of 8 high voltage (1,000 volt) very fast diodes. These components were normally mounted commercially one in a package. They were mesa diodes that were gold doped for speed. A mesa diode means it has an open junction that has to be etched and sealed or the diode can fail. In commercial production a diode is mounted to a package, etched, sealed with a high purity silicone, and then a cap put on the package to hermetically seal the package. At that point it is measured and it is marked to indicate the test results. Another package used 24 smaller diodes that had a lower voltage (400 volt) breakdown and were smaller because they did not have to pass as much current. All the diodes had to have a very low reverse current which was another characteristic that was measured after putting in a package. Both the 8 larger diodes and 24 smaller diodes were wire bonded with one large aluminum wire per device in commercial products.

Ed Massey built us a set up in our laboratory where we could measure the diode chips after etching and storage in dry air. A number of diode chips would have to be etched, measured, and then the open junction sealed with the high purity silicone resin. The diodes that passed our preliminary testing would be bonded to the gold conductor that had been fired on beryllia substrates for good heat conduction. The 1000 volt diodes were then wire bonded with 5 gold wires 0.002 inches in diameter to carry the high current and to spread the current across the surface of the diode instead of concentrating it in one place with one wire. This made the diode more reliable. The beryllia substrates had construction similar to the ATS modules previously described although everything was a much larger substrate. As I recall the dimensions were about 3 inches long by 1.5 inches wide, and 1/8 inch thick. The large copper leads to carry the high current were harder to form after the wire bonding was done and the alumina cap put on with the special epoxy. Both module were done this way and were unlike anything on the market. The modules to control voltage and provide over current protection were built similar to the ATS modules but were a little bigger. The power diode modules on beryllia dissipated a fair amount of power so had to be mounted to the aluminum frame holding the parts. Holes were made in the printed circuit board and the modules fit in those holes with the leads almost parallel to the board and its connections. If the modules were bonded rigidly to the aluminum the difference in thermal expansion of the beryllia and aluminum would cause fracture of the brittle beryllia substrate. Bob Christiansen developed a process using a thin layer of Kapton^c tape having an adhesive backing. The tape was applied to the bottom of the substrate carefully to eliminate air bubbles and then the taped module was bonded to the beryllia substrate with a thermally conductive epoxy. This unique process provided excellent thermal conductivity and it did not deteriorate when subjected to 1,000 thermal cycles from -40°C to +125°C. The control modules were made in a similar fashion to the ATS modules but were larger and I would estimate about 1 inch square.

We made about 50 production computer units and about 10 additional spares with these power supplies. The intended application was the B-52G and B52-H versions. They worked very well I understand and several years later the US Air Force decided they would like some more to retrofit more B-52s and/or other planes but by then the lab had been disbanded and I was in Boulder, Colorado on another assignment. The US Air Force said no one they could find in the country said they had the technology to build power supplies as we had done.

Since we were known for high frequency module design we were asked by the IBM Components Division to build some modules for their test machines. The computer chips had gotten so fast that the test equipment was not able to test them. These were the Duchess class of chips. The test engineers decided that what they needed were high speed modules placed on the test probes to run faster than the new Duchess chips and to buffer the signals and amplify them and send them through the long cables to the test computers. We built several designs that Ed Massey's team came up with and shipped a fairly low quantity (maybe 100 of each type to East Fishkill, New York where the chips were being tested. They worked well we were told. About a year later we were getting orders from other locations for the modules and we did not understand why. It seems the East Fishkill test engineers put our designs in an IBM components book like they were a regular product. We started to get orders as if we were an off the shelf component producer. The ordering engineers did not realize all the special circuits we had made for the test equipment were just that; specials to get the test people out of a problem and we had no intent to supply these parts forever which happens when there is an IBM part number and it is put in a design book. After making a few more parts to get people out of problem we made it clear the parts were not to be obtained from us and the orders stopped.

A fun project we pulled off was to make an advanced technology computer that would execute System 360 instructions and was called HTC or High Technology Computer and a scanned copy of the brochure is included in the Reference section. The computer was unique in that it eliminated as many connectors as possible connectors tend to be a source of unreliability. There were input and output connectors at the box level, but a continuous Kapton^c tape cable with printed circuitry was used to connect all the logic and power supply modules by molding the cable into all the MIBs. The unit was supported in an open position during testing and then folded up like an accordion when test were complete. This was very unique at the time and was another example of the advanced technology present in IBM. The HTC used the tape cables and MLBs from IBM FSD Owego, power supply technology described earlier on the B-52 bombing computer, the semiconductor memory modules of the IBM Components Division, and multi-layer thick film substrates from IBM FSD Huntsville to connect IBM Components Division Duchess technology logic chips that used flip chip solder bump technology. This latter was unique because the Duchess technology had very low "drive" or output power and was used only for single chip SLT modules in the IBM Components Division.

As you can see by one of the pictures in the HTC brochure included in this book IBM FSD Huntsville successfully packaged up to 5 Duchess chips on one substrate and they worked successfully. The difference was that the multi-layer ceramic substrates used in the Components Division used a high temperature ink (molybdenum mix I believe) because the ceramics were "green" sheet and fired at much higher temperature than the thick film multi-layer used by IBM FSD Huntsville. The co-fired ceramic technology used by the Components Division was much more difficult to work with and they made much larger ceramics in the later computers. They had to control not only the purity of the alumina powder but the temperature and humidity of the room where they mixed the alumina with vinyl resin used as a carrier. The shrinkage was quite significant and had to be taken into account as circuit lines were designed. It was a very sophisticated and expensive process not matched by the rest of the world for several years. The production quantities that IBM FSD dealt with were much lower than the commercial world and could not justify the expense of the more sophisticated Components Division process. The Duchess product line manager in the Components Division was Charlie Wolfe who used to work in Owego although I did not know him well. He made the chips available to us. His name will come up again.

I am repeating a story here that I had written about in Chapter 6 if you missed it in the 4Pi section. It is significant enough I think to repeat as it shows that quality control was not always as it should be, most probably on any program and is a reason checks and balances should require independent verification.

By the time the shuttle was being designed and the AP-101S computers being designed in FSD Owego I was in Huntsville, Alabama at IBM and the manager of a hybrid circuit laboratory. We did development of multi-layer thick film ceramic modules, special high performance circuits, and special circuits that allegedly could not be built by others in the industry. At one point we were asked to build some special circuits NOT to be used on the shuttle (we were not NASA man rated certified). These special circuits were to be used to check out the shuttle electronics because the supplier building the production parts was way behind schedule. I was very concerned that the modules we were building would be used for test and possibly find their way into flight equipment as I am skeptical of controls of equipment. I was aware that non-certified parts painted international orange were found in a Titan ballistic missile computer at Cape Kennedy which were working fine, but found when a technician on the launch pad took the covers off the computer to replace a faulty part (not the non-certified) and found the orange painted modules. International orange is that bright orange you see on Coast Guard ships and aircraft because of its high visibility.

The Titan story was told to me by Hugh McNeill who was an Air Force officer and told me this happened at Cape Kennedy. The computer was in a Titan missile to undergo a test launch with production hardware. The computer had some kind of problem (eventually found not to be in the international painted unqualified modules) and had to be removed while the missile was on the launch pad. To delay a launch while many ships and aircraft were at sea in the launch window cost many millions of dollars a day and no one wanted to be responsible for a launch delay. So when the command center queried all the facilities involved Hugh's experienced commander declared the missile was ready to go. Hugh was amazed because the computer was removed on the gantry, covers off it, and they were waiting for a replacement! Hugh's commander knew others might very well not be ready so he was playing a game of chicken. Sure enough as the command center continued their querying a distant radar site said they were not and it would cause a delay. This gave Hugh and his commander sufficient time to get a replacement computer, have the technicians install it, put the cover on the missile where the computer was located and checked it out. The Cape was not responsible for the delay.

We made the special circuit modules in Huntsville and painted them the bright international orange and marked them as non-flight as well as the part number. We built the modules for test about 1977. After the Challenger disaster in 1986 NASA and contractors investigated all the hardware on the ground to make sure all of it was flight ready and of the correct quality. By 1986 I was in Austin, Texas at IBM after a 4 year stay at IBM in Boulder, Colorado. I was called while in Austin, Texas, again managing a special hybrid circuit laboratory, and asked if I remember building some special modules for the space shuttle. Yes I did remember that. Well an examination of some IBM flight hardware had found some bright orange modules made at IBM Huntsville. The caller urgently asked "They were flight qualified, right?" and I answered no that is why they are painted international orange. He tried to get me to say they were flight certified and I refused to go along. The modules were evidently put in for test and worked fine for years and no one noticed and they may very well have worked fine in flight, but I was not going to say we were certified for that part when we were not. Amazing that bright orange parts in 2 instances that I am aware of did not raise attention when in equipment as long as it was working fine. That is scary!

IBM FSD won the bid to provide computer systems and power supplies for the BQQ-5 attack submarines which ran a 5 processor parallel computer (remember the Liberator development at Raytheon?) data cruncher to handle the large amount of data produced by the sonar arrays. IBM was to supply 125, 100 amp 5 volt power supplies with only a couple of spares for each submarine. The total weapons system was very complex and IBM integrated one system per year at a base in Rhode Island. Think of the scenes in the movie "Hunt for the Red October". The power supplies were mounted to copper plates with cooling liquid running through them to provide the cooling to keep the semiconductors quite cool for reliability. IBM delivered 120 systems in the 1980s with revenue over $1B year! The power supplies were so reliable (thought by many in the industry to be unobtainable) that seldom was a spare ever needed on the long undersea deployments.

A control module for the BQQ-5 power supplies was designed for thick film hybrid circuit technology and made at IBM FSD Huntsville. The control modules were to be shipped to IBM FSD Owego for assembly into the power supplies. The module build went reasonably well, but the quantities were controlled by Owego manufacturing that used computer programs to generate part numbers and quantities and then individual orders would be placed for the parts. Owego would continually put in rush expedited orders for parts periodically and claim that Huntsville was not reacting quickly enough causing us a great deal of unnecessary grief. The Huntsville plant manager would 'jump" all over us because he was getting criticized by executives in Owego as this was an important revenue generating program.

After getting "chewed out" several times with no chance of logical rebuttal I found out that the rush orders were happening because the manufacturing computer generation had "crashed" and no parts could be ordered until they got a good generation. A production engineering part generation could be a big stack of 140 column computer paper. Since one module was needed per power supply and they were building an average of 105 per month what was the big deal. So with my usual diplomatic way I wrote a message (we had an early version of email at IBM much before the industry did) to some IBM management at Owego. The question I had was why someone in manufacturing was not smart enough to multiply one by the number of power supplies to be built and send us an order? Or, send us a standing order for one module times the number of power supplies to be built ahead of time? There was some consternation about my impudence, but once they thought how silly they would look if this went up the corporate chain we started to get hand orders on a regular schedule that allowed us to meet all requirements on normal time and stop working nights and weekends because they were stupid. Common sense is hard to get to sometimes in our computer world of today.

Chapter 9
Ink Jet Laboratory

As the manufacturing in IBM FSD Huntsville was coming to an end IBM generously offered to transfer employees to other locations and pay the moving expenses. This was extremely different from the move from Thousand Oaks, California where people were encouraged to quit and were not treated very well at all. This was an anomaly that got IBM a lot of bad press inside the company and outside of the company. The move from Huntsville they went the other way and the company went out of their way to accommodate people. They even had a corporate ombudsman and it was a man I knew, Arden Wolterman. I said I would like to go to Boulder, Colorado as the family liked it when we went to Colorado on vacation. Plants were told they would get people from Huntsville and they had to find them jobs which was not well received by the plants, but they were not given choices. After I made my choice I was told I could not transfer because I was too valuable and would have to go back to Owego, New York where I joined the company. I and the family were not very happy as we had done our time in Owego. After I made an appointment with Arden Wolterman and we talked a bit he asked me where I wanted to go and I said Boulder, Colorado. He said, "you got it." and that was it.

When I arrived in Boulder I was to report to Tom Young (MS in Optics) and to manage a small department making very fine precision glass nozzles for ink jet computers. IBM had tried a number of ways to make small precision holes to eject ink through. One was to etch holes in silicon, but the holes came out four sided as I recall and not round because of the crystal structure. The idea was to integrate the electrical stimulation to "pump" the ink in precise droplets. Great idea but IBM Yorktown research could not get that to work. Another was to drill holes by using a spade drill in a air turbine small machine but getting the drills was expensive and breakage was frequent (imagine drill 0.001 inches which is less thick than a human hair). Laser drilling was tried at the time (1977) in metals, glass, and ceramic but clean precise repeatable holes did not result. Yorktown came up with a special glass that was ink resistant and a machine that took glass tubing made with that glass and then heated the tubing and pulled it to a finer tube that was very accurate on the inside diameter. By accurate I mean to several wavelengths of light! Boulder was given the machine and people had learned how to operate it . I was told the operation and my immediate job was to transfer the knowledge from Yorktown to Boulder to make Boulder independent so it would be possible to go into production if everything was successful.

The concept was to package 168 of these small tubes precisely in glass plates that has grooves cut in them, lay the tubes carefully into the grooves, and then I think the assembly was finalized by putting a glass plate on top and using a lower melting point glass to join the lower plate, tubes, and upper plate. When the small blocks with the 168 tubes enclosed was completed the block was turned 90 degrees and the block cut into very thin slices. The slices were then resin bonded to a precision metal plate. That metal plate would be attached to another metal plate with a cavity which was stimulated by a piezoelectric crystal. The crystal would pulse from computer control and this would make precision droplets of ink pushed out of the 168 nozzles at the same time. With the crystal oscillating at a high rate there would be a continuous stream of droplets being emitted. This was all under way before I arrived in Boulder. The department making the tubing, machining the glass plates, joining the tubing to the plates and then machining into thin slices, and bonding them to a metal plate was to be my responsibility.

Gary Fillmore (PhD in Information Theory) managed the department that worked on the cavity design, piezoelectric crystal stimulation, and successfully helped design the ink cavity valve by doing a basic analog solution. Gary's department also measured the experimental nozzle patterns emitted. Another member of the team was Jerry Lammers who had a PhD in aerodynamics and his job was to design the shrouding around the nozzles to direct the air stream resulting in 168 straight lines. The ink being pumped out caused the outer nozzles to move ink streams toward the center by moving air as the ink was pumped. The concept of this ink jet printer was to emit the drops for short distance in very straight lines and to raster them by electrical charge in precise small moves much like a cathode ray tube directs electron beams to make an image on the phosphor coated glass screen. When an ink drop was not wanted the charge would be regulated so the ink drop would land in a gutter and not be deposited on the paper in the printer. A number of 168 nozzle print heads would be in the machine some having color inks and a black ink. The resultant printer/copier was supposed to be capable of of several dozen copies per minute. The control of the electrical scanning of a document or buffering of image data in the copier/printer was in a department managed by William Althauser.

As you can tell this was quite a technical challenge to put it all together and I was only a small part of that. The first thing I learned was on a tour of the glass making facility led by a Yorktown engineer and the specialty glass maker manager. I think the glass maker was Anchor Hocking but I am not sure except it was not Corning which I would have expected. IBM had to pay for a platinum lined special glass crucible to melt the special glass and corporate security was always concerned that many thousands of dollars of platinum was in a ceramic crucible not on IBM property. When IBM ordered tubing they had to order quite a bit of it as the crucible produced pounds of glass in order to have a good mixture. The glass maker would deliver tubing in lengths of about 2 feet as I recall but that is foggy. The glass tubing delivered was about 1/4 inch in outer diameter and perhaps 1/16 inch inside diameter. Sorry but this is pretty foggy too as it has been over 35 years ago.

I think I had limited contribution to the ink nozzle making. I did make a special effort to justify a Japanese Disco diamond wheel precision machine that was very accurate in 3 dimensions using an internal laser measuring system. These machines were typically used to cut silicon wafers into individual silicon die and were expensive. However, the procurement of the machine I was familiar with having worked on semiconductors really helped and a machinist and die maker Richard Erickson made very precision glass plates and slices of joined glass blocks with the nozzles. The only thing I did was to come up with a scheme to identify every nozzle slice that was required by corporate security since this was a secret project. Every nozzle slice had to be accounted for every night in a book and any nozzles not being used had to be locked up in a safe. Marking nozzle plates would be time consuming and risk damaging the nozzles. I came up with a scheme where before slicing the assembled blocks Rich would machine very fine slots at the top of the assemblies at a 0.05 inch spacing as I recall (the machine would allow multiple diamond saws to be put on the spindle by using precision spacers). The assembly would be put at a precise angle and as the machine cut it would make a series of parallel slots. When the block was cut into very thin slices the slots would appear at the top at different distances from the left edge and with a magnifying glass and precision machinist ruler the distances could be measured from the edge resulting in a digital code that could be recorded as a number. Therefore every slice was individually identifiable.

By leaving a specific diamond saw out of a location would identify what block the slices had come from. This was simple and required no special equipment to identify a specific nozzle, block, and with that record it could be traced back to a manufacturing date with process information.

One problem experienced with resin bonding the nozzle slices to the metal plate was the ink which was alkaline eventually degraded the bond and the slice would fall off with the pressure of the ink being emitted. There was a process used by San Jose to join a different type of glass assembly. Called Mallory bonding after the patent two very flat glass surfaces could be joined by intimate contact and a high voltage. Glass containing enough sodium would be transported or migrated across the surfaces and join the glass. After looking at that process it did not appear attractive for us because it required too much sodium. Remembering my textile background I was aware it was hard to bond to glass with a resin. The way fiberglass textiles were made and fiber treated for composite structures was to pre-treat the glass with a very polar organic made by Union Carbide. We bought some and mixed with water of various pH levels to determine the optimum mixture. We tested by putting glass in the mixtures, bonding, and immersing in ink samples. Although there was skepticism about the process a number of nozzle slices were treated with the solution, epoxy bonded, and were successful as ink nozzles as a good bond was made between the glass and resin.

When I was assigned to the ink jet laboratory at Boulder IBM was still in relatively good shape financially (not if you looked at cash flow as I had a tendency to do) and many employees at every level were used to increases and promotions at a very fast rate which happened through the 1960s and 1970s with the growth of the corporation. I had some employees assigned to me that wanted to get promoted and that was a hot subject with them. In a department meeting I told them that if they really wanted a promotion I thought I could help get most of them a promotion in a year if they wanted. Tom Young and Gary Fillmore thought I had gone over the edge and were not sure about this guy from FSD. I pointed out to the people in the department that as individuals we are much more in charge of our life than we wanted to admit and when things did not happen there was a tendency to blame "them". Whoever that is.

So I asked them if they would like to transfer to another plant. Not much of a response there. Did they want to transfer to another division. Not a lot of response there either. How about a transfer to manufacturing. Not a lot of enthusiasm for that. How about just a transfer out of the department. A little more thought but people liked it where they were. My point was the department could not justify promotions for everyone in the department, and they were doing the decision making to not get promoted not me. There are opportunities but very limited in our department.

Some people thought it over and changed their mind. Art Hoffman approached me and he was willing to transfer to another plant and with his talent and a little help from me he was offered a promotion in Burlington, VT and left. A technician named Dave (cannot remember his last name) changed his mind and was willing to go to another engineering department that needed his skills and he was promoted by that manager on the transfer. Richard Erickson wanted to stay where he was and was willing to stay at his level, a good one, for now. Joe Moss was a capable technician but needed help in writing reports and communicating effectively in my view before I would go before a promotion board and recommend him. He was really mad at me, but was willing to take some writing courses that IBM offered for free and to start writing the department reports with my help and learn to give presentations on his work to others. Joe worked hard and did well and I recommended him for a promotion which was granted in about a year. Joe was very proud and said if I promoted him no one could say he did not earn it. But isn't that what all of us want? To be recognized for earning something and not getting a gift we might not deserve. Too many people were promoted in IBM to satisfy them and when the downsizings came the managers they reported to lowered their ratings and they were the first to go. That was very harmful to the person and to the corporation also when the larger picture is looked at. People who were capable should have been told the truth and encouraged and shown how to develop their skills (IBM had great employee education opportunities) or helped to find jobs where their talents were the strongest.

When the family and I moved to Boulder we lived in an area known as Gunbarrel Greens which was very nice and not far from the IBM plant. We had the lowest cost house in the area and the plant manager lived across the street from us and the University of Colorado basketball coach lived 2 houses away and my daughter Lori baby sat for the children some time. I think it was less than a year after we moved IBM transferred the team that made disk drives to Tucson, Arizona and houses became available. We looked at a large house on the western ridge of the foothills on north Boulder known as Boulder Heights and we bought that house while still owning the house in Boulder. Thank goodness the house in Boulder sold quickly at a slight profit. The large house (for us) in the foothills was about 5,000 square feet with a walk out basement and was like living in a resort as we could look out from our deck and living room at Long's Peak on the Continental Divide. We were against some of the Roosevelt National Forest so there were deer, bear, and at least one goshawk that scared the heck out of me once. In the summer I cut pine trees down and cut lower limbs off of pine trees to minimize fire risk and with the thinning of the trees per the county directions none died of the pine beetle because they all had enough water. Flowers and grasses grew where the pine trees were cut. The children were of the age that they could slide down our woods road in the winter snow and have friends over. The walk out basement had a fireplace and indoor/outdoor carpet along with a utility room, dark room, and full bath so it was great easy fun. I cut and split a lot of wood for our fireplace. It was a good time and I jogged about 35 miles a week and was working only 5 days a week which was quite a change from FSD. I was in the Office Product Division (OPD) that made copiers and above all the revenue producing Selectric typewriters.

Then I got a call from Ed Massey who wanted me to come to Austin, Texas where he was working for OPD and to form a hybrid circuit laboratory and where there was a plan to build a surface mount assembly line for PCs. Remember the Saturn V program with ULDs? Using all surface mount components was now a popular way to make electronic consumer products and IBM wanted to go all in. Ed came to Boulder with Charlie Powers his manager who enthusiastically described his vision of an all surface mount assembly line and how he wanted me to come to Austin. Ed admitted they didn't have a lot of tall trees in Austin like Colorado and it could get very hot, but he really wanted me to come. I told Ed and Charlie that the only way I would go voluntarily was to be promoted to Senior Engineer. IBM at that time frowned on promotions to get people to move as they felt it had been overused and it probably was, but that was my price. Ed and Charlie went back to Austin and talked to Tom Lewis who originally came out of FSD. Tom was reluctant about promoting this gangly kid to Senior Engineer but relented. Perhaps Ed told him about my contribution on ATS when I was in Huntsville and Tom Lewis was in charge of the ATS program at IBM Gaithersburg, Maryland and the program was in trouble. Whatever the total reason Charlie and Ed got me the promotion and I moved to Austin on January 2, 1981 and I have been in Texas ever since. John my oldest had moved to Huntsville, Alabama after graduating from Boulder high, but moved back to Boulder and was working after a brief stay at the University of Alabama at Huntsville. Lori was a senior in high school and wanted to graduate from Boulder High as you can imagine and so I moved to Austin in January and the family moved in June of

1981. That fall Lori started her nursing study at Baylor in Waco, Texas and David started the 6th grade as I recall in the Round Rock Independent School District. We chose that because a special ed teacher I found that was dedicated to technology for the blind and already had a blind student. We chose to buy a home in Round Rock where Fabia Smith would teach David to finish elementary school, then middle school, and the high school. We did this by studying the school boundaries for different neighborhoods, and we purchased a house where Fabia would be teaching David in all schools.

Chapter 10
Hybrid Circuits & Worldwide Manufacturing

I am not sure why, but my recollections at Austin are not as good as some of the prior experiences and I will say up front that in my mind I have confused the two laboratories with details of employees of each and for that I apologize.

By the time I arrived in Austin the plans and equipment for the all surface mount assembly line was well under way. This was a very advanced idea for the time outside of Japan that had embraced miniaturization in a big way. Consumer items like Sony's Walkman and very small video cameras and Olympus' shrinking film cameras are examples. Consumer products like personal computers were large and the size was driven mostly by the use of through hole technology where all the components had leads inserted into holes in the circuit boards and soldered. Where Charlie Power's vision would lead would be what we see as laptops and tablets today, but the components suppliers were not ready for such a drastic change and that really hurt the program. Another thing that hurt was the lack of manufacturing vision in IBM for versatility and flexibility. Lines were designed for very high volumes of the same part and unfortunately the board designs were changing frequently to use advancing technology. IBM could compete if the volumes were high enough for a single part number. Eventually the lines at Austin changed to more flexible lines similar to the sub-contract manufacturing suppliers but that is another story.

So my first assignment was to design a hybrid circuit laboratory that could produce prototypes of production circuits to be made elsewhere. The mission was to help the Office Products Division (OPD) shrink equipment like their word processor which was the first or one of the first products on the market dedicated to replacing the typewriter. It had a large floppy disk for memory and with programs it could be sold to offices wanting to keep records without paper, be able to make revisions without typing all over again, and where repeated forms were used like legal offices. OPD was doing reasonably well in the area but wanted to go to smaller machines. Ed Massey, Gus Schrottke, and Denny Oliver were doing electrical design in Austin and Ed was my manager.

The laboratory space was in a leased building off IBM property (on Braker Lane) but near it in north Austin (Burnet Road) where the large manufacturing plant and engineering offices were. The largest printed circuit board plant in the world was there making boards for several divisions of IBM. Across Burnet Road on the east side a large complex was built for programmers. Today I believe that all the manufacturing buildings on the west side have been sold and may not even be operating.

The laboratory had an high temperature belt oven room, a laser trimming room, a small wire bonding area, and a small solder and assembly area. Storage for semi-conductors started out using dry nitrogen and changed to dry (-51^0C) air. We had an equipment room that housed the air dryer, air compressor, and electrical switches for master power. We had a 50 Kilowatt emergency generator outside the equipment room that would automatically switch on if the power was lost from the commercial grid. Ken Rhyner was one designer and had been working at Texas Instruments he was working at Texas Instruments in the Dallas, Texas area in 2014. Jim Honeycutt had transferred from Huntsville to Austin when Huntsville was downsizing and I went to Boulder. So Jim was welcomed into the hybrid laboratory in charge of wire bonding again as was Tom Battle who had also transferred to Austin.

One of the first modules I remember was a power supply control module. The power design was very innovative as a control module was designed by the circuit designers that had common circuitry for various voltages and currents, and once the module was assembled, but the cap not yet put on a laser would trim key resistors. That trimming controlled the voltage and how much current would be allowed (fold back current). So if a short occurred the current would automatically fold back or reduce to prevent damage to the supply or the control module. This meant that modules could be partially assembled, stored safely, taken out and customized for an application, and then capped and part marked. It was a very clever design I thought.

A minute here about trimming thick film resistors. With abrasive trimming under a microscope one could see tiny black resistor particles on the white alumina substrates and if you looked carefully at circuit performance those particles would cause noise. Also, the abrasive powder would leave rough edges which also could cause noise. By changing the width to length ratio of the trim in the typical rectangular resistor you could change the inductance component. When the laser trimmers became available they were very fast compared to the abrasive trimmers but would leave an ionized plume of vaporized particles which would be part of the measuring circuit as it was being trimmed to a target resistance. So, it was better on precision trims to due a rough trim, pause for a few seconds, and then do a final trim. Again, the length and width ratio of the trim would affect the inductance component. Why mention all of this? Because it was one example of the many variables that laboratory personnel working with the circuit designers could cooperate to make the best circuits possible. It was not just hacking away some material and changing the resistance. There were similar but important subtleties in resistor to conductor interface, wire bonding intermetallics with the semiconductors, intermetallic interfaces with solder joints, and many others. I would like to think with our combined talent why we were able to make reliable parts that performed better than were typically available on the open market.

One part I think led to our downfall in the eyes of the Austin product designers and therefore our support by management. That was called the Power Hybrid Driver (PHD). This part was to be a pin through hole (PTH) part that had several power parts made by Unitrode which was a power semiconductor manufacturer in Massachusetts. In the laboratory we made some parts in hybrid thick film that were fairly simple electrically, but challenging to put that much power in a small dual in line package (DIP) which was a PTH common shape. The power components were mounted to heavier than normal copper leads (to take away the heat and put it into the board) that were high temperature bonded to the copper leads. The diode and transistor were wire bonded with a thick aluminum wire of about 0.005 inch diameter. To keep the cost low the part was to be molded with plastic instead of hermetic sealing with a cap. Unitrode was chosen to be the production supplier since the semiconductors used was theirs. The main designer at Unitrode had not worked on a multi-chip or hybrid module and was quite experienced but set in his ways. He did not take recommendations well like to put radiused notches in the leads near the body of the part so the leads would form easier and not crack the plastic molding during bending. They were notched but not as much as they needed to be in our opinion. Things were not going well and our project manager in manufacturing Ed Linde wanted to put the best face on things, and we reached a point where I worried the non-delivery of a good part would hurt product release so I went around Ed as he would not reveal the extent of our problems. It was hard to do as he was a nice guy, but things were out of hand.

The problem was looked into by others and the program at Unitrode was killed and product electrical designers had to work very hard to get a small board designed that would replace the PHD component. They were not happy. Manufacturing management was not happy. Ed was not happy with me. No one was happy. It was not a good time and I believe that was the beginning of the end of the hybrid laboratory despite the talent there and potential. It demonstrated that without complete control over an advanced product that success is very risky. I could have continued working with an obstinate supplier and not said anything, but not to do so would most probably delay the word processing product and hurt revenue and I would rather have people mad at me than cost the company millions of dollars in lost revenue. If I was wrong others would have picked up the banner after removing me and gone on. No one volunteered to do that.

I cannot remember (probably not happy so the memories are swept away) a lot of the details but Ed Massey went to work for Education which was a waste of his talent I believe. I found a spot in a worldwide manufacturing organization called a PMC which I think stands for Product Management Center or something. In any case the PMC reported to corporate manufacturing and was responsible for doing financial analyses of equipment mix for production lines, ensuring product qualifications on printed circuit boards was being done correctly worldwide and helping select worldwide sub-contractors or IBM plants for printed circuit board assembly. I had never worked in a group like that and it was interesting to say the least. The financial men I met were top class and felt as I did that fixed assembly lines were only perfect when one part number was made in high volumes. That is not the electronics assembly business. Flexible and fast on your feet and yes sometimes equipment is not 100% utilized but that is not as important as the flexibility and quick reaction time where a 6 month time in the market with something new is when you make your money. After 6 months the imitators are chasing you and cutting cost to the bone. Don Cooper headed up the PMC and was hard set on the fixed line concept so you can see we had some differences. He was authoritarian and so the finance guys and I went about our business of doing the best we could for the product lines within our limits.

My first manager in the PMC was John Reynolds who was a procurement manager and had recently come back from living in Hong Kong as I recall and had traveled extensively in China (this is about 1988) when traveling was really primitive. He was doing work to advise the IBM Corporation on future manufacturing possibilities and markets. In my opinion he should have headed up the PMC but maybe he did not make PowerPoint presentations as good as Don. IBM at the corporate level at that time was so bureaucratic and autocratic they thought the world revolved around Westchester County and them. There were people with the responsibility of choosing the fonts and colors of presentations to the top executives. John Reynolds was not only experienced and smart he was a gentle insightful man you listened to and learned. If he thought you knew what you were doing he gave you an assignment and let you go. No micro-managing like Cooper.

After John Reynolds got another assignment I reported to John Darnaby who had been the manager of Austin IBM procurement for over 5 years when the average life of that assignment was about a year.

Procurement managers in IBM that I knew had killing assignments. John Darnaby like John Reynolds was an experienced hand and let people do their jobs once he knew they were capable. On several trips to SCI (a large sub-contractor of IBM PC assemblies) I learned a lot. The CEO of SCI in Huntsville, Alabama was a hard charging arrogant man who gave us a lecture on how smart they were and how dumb IBM manufacturing was. IBM Boca Raton responsible for the IBM PC product line had given SCI several very large contracts. We were suspicious that once the PMC took over contract responsibility the Boca Raton procurement manager retired and went to work for SCI. I will not speculate any more, but a reasonable person can draw their own conclusions. SCI was smart and cheap they claimed but every time there was a process problem IBM engineers had to go solve it and audits of their quality showed they were not up to IBM standards over and over again. SCI eventually (after lucrative IBM contracts went away) they went down hill and an Italian assembly machine company bought most of their facilities. John Darnaby and I made several trips to SCI in Huntsville where I would do the looking around and the report the discrepancies to John who handled it from there. I did not mind traveling to Huntsville as my oldest son John and his family were there as well as the Space Museum and I could point out things I worked on to John.

The IBM Corporation has national companies where they operate with national managers with national allegiances. So we went to IBM Scotland's manufacturing facility in Greenock near Glasgow they were good and knew it and did not "cotton" to us Americans coming to tell them how to do things or perhaps take away some of their work and ship it to another plant which the PMC could have great influence in. I became friends with one of those sharp engineers Brian Pereira and we have kept in touch and he and his wife have very nicely toured us for a day twice when we visited Scotland. The biggest worry that Greenock had was not their quality or engineering expertise it was keeping as much production as possible to keep their plant busy and not have the PMC recommend to move some of it. I did a lecture one afternoon on ball grid array assembly to PCBs to their engineers and how to make reliable solder joints with the new products coming out for the PowerPC CPUs.

I went with the Scotland nationals to 2 electronic board assembly companies in the corridor between Greenock and Edinburgh. They were international companies already in to technology that could make suitable parts for IBM Scotland with oversight of Greenock engineers.

Another foreign plant I visited a couple of times was the Vimercate, Italy plant north of Milan about 65 miles. Again, the engineers were good and the quality was good. They were fairly busy but anticipated more orders than they could handle at the plant, and the plant management wanted the PMC assistance in choosing a supplier to bring up to IBM standards of quality. The task was to investigate potential suppliers to start surface mount electronic assembly which was generally not known in Europe where most PCB assemblies were done with PTH technology and equipment. I visited one plant in L'Aquila (being in the central mountains the town name means the eagle or designating an eagle's nest) later (2009) it suffered much damage in an earthquake which is in an area of damaging earthquakes over centuries. It has some beautiful Roman plazas and architectural monuments of note. It is east of Rome and about 65 miles north of Rome. The telephone equipment company we looked at was way behind in technology and the president of it reminded me of Mussolini in build and manner.

Some of their engineers were trying to get into surface mount technology (SMT) or mixed SMT and PTH boards, but knew they were way behind. I did not recommend them.

We went by car to the Venice area and looked at another potential supplier, and they were somewhat better than the telephone equipment supplier but would need a lot of attention to make IBM assemblies. I was fortunate to travel with nationals and luckily they spoke English well as I had no more than a few survival words based on my boyhood Latin. Some considerable time and review went into looking at the IBM qualification of SMT and mixed SMT and PTH technology at Vimercate. It was my opinion that they were qualified after hours of review of the tests and details of the results.

The PMC and Don Cooper was criticized by plant managers who wanted to manage their own business and get more flexible. The PMC concept was looked at as an overhead cost and bureaucracy that was questioned in large parts of the corporation. There were PMCs for a number of IBM manufacturing technologies or product types. It was death by a thousand razor cuts.

In the summer of 1991 IBM offered a buyout to IBM employees who wanted to retire early or to retire fully if they were eligible. The desire was to reduce the number of people who were older and making more money and I am sure thought to be obsolete which was true in many cases. I was eligible for full retirement with IBM's formula and said I would go and after I filled out my papers I was told I was too valuable and could not take advantage of the offer which was a year's pay and medical benefits for life. Of course no one could keep me from retiring but they could withhold the year's pay. I appealed as the notice from corporate did not say there were restrictions. Sounded like Huntsville where I was so valuable. I felt the atmosphere of the management of IBM was biased against anyone over 45. A whole department retired from Endicott when they were told they were obsolete (tool and die makers).

Then IBM found they had no one left to make precision tooling. The ex-employees set up their own company with their own funding and started a tool and die machine shop. Soon IBM set aside all their rules on not doing business for a year with ex-employees and became the new shop's best customers. Now IBM was paying them full retirement and the new company's salaries. Hiring back experienced employees happened when IBM found too much knowledge had left. Hiring the term "consultants" became a naughty word so they hired the people back as independent contractors. I was held for 60 days from retiring with my year's pay bonus while I allegedly was to transfer SMT to IBM Charlotte, North Carolina a plant I had refused a transfer to earlier as I felt was on the way out from a manufacturing viewpoint. When I went to Charlotte for several days to explain the material in the several storage boxes I had pre-shipped there was no one there to teach. The morale was very low. IBM sold the manufacturing plant to an outside firm with the IBM employees that IBM had transferred there for "new opportunities". It was obviously planned all the time.

While I was in Austin I was asked to be one of the engineers evaluating patent disclosures to see if they should be pursued. I saw so many that were not new in my view that I was removed. The US law says an idea should not be obvious to one skilled in the art or words to that effect. The reason for my removal according a patent attorney was I was "too expert". I am not sure how you can be "too expert", but evidently I was. Remember this if you read about my time at Motorola.

A task I enjoyed was being asked to develop the curriculum and find IBM instructors to teach a one week course in Westchester County at an IBM education center in surface mount technology for IBM engineers worldwide. I had the good fortune to know many of the people that I thought would make good instructors for specific tasks or I knew the managers to ask to get some of the best people already in surface mount technology. The class was all classroom and no laboratory if you will, but engineers were invited to various plants to get hands on experience if they wanted to do that. Everyone was given copies of the presentations which was a considerable package and most just shipped them back to their home plants instead of carrying them. The class ran as I recall for 4 times in a little over a year and was well received and by then most plants with a surface mount mission were up and running. A side benefit for many if not most of the attendees was the contacts they made with fellow IBM engineers and they could contact experts in their field or fellow engineers working on the same product type to share information.

Before I left Austin I was asked to go back to Boulder to review a program and give my input. As I recall I was not on a team but knew most of the engineers and unlike the experience at Endicott I wrote about earlier this was a lot more straightforward and I felt that most of the engineers had come to the same conclusion I ended up with, but the management had not been paying a lot of attention. So basically like a consultant I listened and told me what I heard and told them an answer they already knew. Not much value add I don't think, but it was nice to see Tom Young and Gary Fillmore again.

My time was up at IBM and I retired at the end of September 1991 on a Friday and started at Motorola on Monday as a design manager. The senior manager speaking up to hire me? Charlie Wolfe of ex IBM FSD and Duchess renown. That is the start of another story.

Chapter 11
My Time With Motorola

When I went to Motorola part of the employment process was to take a drug test (passed that) and a hearing test (failed miserably). I did not understand why I had to take the hearing test as I would not be working on a manufacturing line subjected to possible loud noises. They did it for everyone. The nurse asked me if I ever shot high powered rifles, operated a chain saw, operated a gasoline powered weed trimmer, ever been around race cars, and the like and the answers to all was yes. She said, "No wonder you are partially deaf then.".

I started at a salary about 75% of what I was making at IBM which was acceptable to me as they did not know what they were getting. Charlie Wolfe the ex-IBM FSD and IBM Duchess program manager had hired me after a recommendation from some other IBMers. I was not his first choice to be honest as he did not have a recent memory of me, but after checking me out with contacts at IBM and an interview he started the hiring process. Motorola had a different kind of compensation program. Up to a certain level you got a salary and increases that could be recommended (and usually approved) by your immediate manager. I was brought in close to the top of the level. To be considered for a higher salary you had to go on a pure management track (hard to do at a new company) or after one year you could apply for the Technical Ladder. The Technical Ladder was for engineers or engineering managers only and people on the Technical Ladder voted on whom they knew and rated them in a number of technical areas. To prevent or inhibit people voting high for their friends or each other a senior technical man would review the high results in each plant and he could overturn obvious cheating on the voting. The man at the Austin SemiConductor Products Division was very well respected and quite stern so you did not want to get on his bad side in a cheating situation.

After one year Charlie really had to persuade me to apply for the ladder as I was quite intimidated as a newcomer from another company and there were several of us ex-IBMers (Joel Dietz, Stuart Greer, and Eric Hubacher in addition to Charlie Wolfe) who had been brought on board to help Motorola be successful as they had bought a license from IBM for IBM's solder bump technology and the PowerPC architecture. The PowerPC architecture used some of System 360 and could be used for CPUs or application oriented special chips which Motorola wanted to design. Motorola, IBM, and Apple had a joint program to design the PowerPC devices and Motorola and IBM would bid against each other for production chip supplies. There was a separate building where the PowerPC team resided and met and meetings were held there for people that did not work in that building all the time. So with a lot of ex-IBM people showing up in semiconductor process technology and packaging there was considerable resentment by some Motorola employees especially the plant manager who was an ex-Marine with a 19th century management style. No wonder I was apprehensive on applying to the Technical Ladder with only one year experience. If you did not get a minimum score it was really bad. If you did not get a score that would have justified your salary level that was bad, if you got a score higher than your present salary level would indicate you could get a good raise or even a promotion and upper management did not have a lot of say in that (made some upper management mad). Well I applied for the ladder (applicants do not get to vote) and luckily got votes (minimum of 10 needed with highest and lowest scores thrown out) high enough to justify my salary and a decent raise. I should say that technical people on the ladder in Austin, Phoenix, Arizona, Scottsdale, Arizona, and Schaumberg, Illinois could vote if they claimed to know you. The marking was on a Gaussian curve so many engineers would be around the midpoint. I was fortunate to be rated higher than the midpoint. By the end of my career I had been promoted twice and was rated as a Technical Staff Member which is where I was at the end of my IBM career, but now I was in a different company. I was eligible for stock options and made a nice 6 figure salary when I retired in August 2001.

The first thing I had to do at Motorola was to meet the people going to report to me. One was Pat Johnson a talented and creative physical designer who understood high speed electrical concerns and another was Jim Casto who also was very talented although his expertise was complex wire bonding layouts as Motorola used wire bonding up to that point. Jim quickly caught on to ball grid array packages where the substrate (at that time ceramic) had solder bump interconnections to the PCB and were designed in a matrix. As time went on Motorola migrated to a lot of organic substrates which were cheaper to make, had more suppliers, and had some challenges as the semiconductor chips expanded a lot less than the organic and could crack under thermal cycling without careful design. Ken Rhyner was a computer aided physical designer and although not an engineer was very good as he had lots of PCB design experience. Ken is now a designer at Texas Instruments in Dallas as I write this.

Motorola had a young engineer, Andrew Mawer, that was very bright and had done a large amount of work in plastic ball grid array (BGA) solder joint reliability. He led a lot of testing by thermal cycling of plastic BGA packages using daisy chain testing with monitoring so if an open joint happened it could be detected and traced. He was very good at using statistical analysis to be able to predict solder joint reliability for customers in their applications. This was similar to the work that Roger Wild and others did at IBM FSD Owego. He was particularly good at using Weibull statistics. Soon he extended his work to include ceramic BGAs that we would use on the PowerPC product line. The ceramic BGAs in that case were multi-layer green sheet cofired ceramics supplied by IBM and for a few parts supplied by Hitachi. The IBM parts were more expensive and better but made it hard to compete against IBM head to head with supplying parts to Apple.

Pat Johnson and Jim Casto did not need any technical help from me as they were very experienced and innovative electronic chip packaging engineers. However, as the PowerPC product line evolved I pushed hard that the power and grounds for families of chips we had plans for in the near future be the same assignments on the bottom of the package. As much as possible common items like clock and the like would have the same connection assignment as the computer chip family was evolving so many of the same functions were already known about the chip. The reason I did the emphasis on pre-assignments, which caused a lot of consternation with IBM as they had to be compatible, was the board designs by Apple and potentially other buyers could be done to accommodate the chip families without new board designs. IBM always did custom boards requiring new tooling and so did not think of the advantages of compatibility and flexibility. Apple and a couple of other buyers saw the advantage immediately. They could design one board for several generations which saved design and lead time, reduced inventory, and meant there would be a lower risk of errors on a new design. Pat and Jim pulled this off well and I can remember at least 3 generations of PowerPC processors that worked on one board design just by adding support chips as necessary for the newer processors. I did not invent this. It was an idea I saw the Japanese doing on consumer products. They would design a board and lay it out for the "full house" function for the highest priced unit and then just remove chips for the lower priced units and maybe some software changes. Fast to market, minimum inventory, and a low cost way to go. In the US the typical method was to have 2 or more designs for 2 to 3 models.

A lot of time was spent on transferring the technology from IBM to Motorola with regards to the details of the device packaging. IBM had gone to a resin injected under the chip after soldering to the ceramic to aid in solder joint life with thermal cycling encountered in turning the devices on and off. This had to be done since semiconductor chips were getting much larger in size which exasperated the problem of the difference in expansion between the silicon semiconductor and the much lower thermal coefficient of expansion of the alumina ceramic. When IBM started System 360 about 1964 there was one transistor per chip and by 1991 there were over 0.5 million transistors per chip and when I retired in 2001 there were over 10 million transistors per chip. In 2014 there were about 150 million transistors per chip and the silicon chips or semiconductor die were as large as 0.5 inches!

In any case some of the IBM engineers that had developed the resin (called underfill) to go under the devices did not like the idea that the IBM Corporation had licensed that technology to Motorola and a bunch of "traitor" ex-IBMers were doing the technology transfer. So getting the right answers was not easy at times. The idea of putting resin under chips to help offset thermal expansion differences and provide environmental protection (corrosion) was a popular subject in the electronics industry since many companies were starting to put bumped chips (bumps were all kind of materials) on PCBs directly on consumer products. So, Motorola was not completely dependent on IBM and eventually this problem faded away.

At one time as Motorola and IBM were competing to supply PowerPC devices to Apple for a laptop we came up with a different conclusion. I had given an input that the reliability would meet Apple's requirements. IBM told Apple that the ceramic BGAs would NOT meet the reliability requirements for solder joint failure. Apple wanting to resolve this called a meeting in Austin at the Motorola facility. Motorola management was very nervous and wanted to know if I was really sure. Yes I was and I wanted to see how IBM came up with a different answer. IBM flew in about 10 people which was typical of them to use numbers to overcome. After some preliminaries IBM had a PhD get up to the white board and show why the ceramic BGA would not work and all the time the pedagogical and arrogance was showing with the IBM members. Their man was the expert. When it was my term I showed them that he had made an error in the Coffin-Manson fatigue factor assumptions of power on/off cycles. The fatigue equation was based on the temperature changes of the solder joint caused by turning the part on and off. As the part was turned on it would heat and expand and transfer that heat to the PCB which would expand but more than the ceramic. When the power was removed the system would cool and this back and forth motion would slowly stress the solder bumps to the point they would break. Up to this point we all agreed. What the expert overlooked as he was used to working with big systems that rarely get turned off and on, was that laptops get turned off and on a lot to save battery power. So, in the equation was a factor of power on/off cycles per day. I argued that a laptop user would most likely use their equipment 10 to 12 hours a day and the most damaging thing would be to turn it on in the morning and off at night, but that is not many cycles. By turning the laptop on and off a lot it was a lot of cycles but the ceramic BGA and the PCB did not have an opportunity to heat and cool very much so the cycles were high but the expansion difference is much smaller. An example would be to turn the laptop on and off every second. The part never has an opportunity to heat the ceramic up and it would last as long as the chip would last which is a very long time. Motorola won. IBM was embarrassed and went home. Apple was impressed. The expert applied for a high level job at Motorola and was turned down.

At Motorola I managed an able team of materials and mechanical engineers doing a lot of customer support on wire bonded ball grid arrays which were well under way before I joined Motorola. The plastic BGAs were very economical and used in many consumer products. We also did projections of reliability of the solder joints of the BGAs by thermal cycling and testing to failure. Andrew Mawer was instrumental in doing the statistical analysis and publishing results. The thermal cycling chambers, failure analysis, building of test parts and the like were all done in the department I managed. Mike McShane was a long term Motorola employee and as organization changes were made I reported to him and he reported to me. Before I left Motorola Mike want to work in the Intellectual Property department of Motorola which became a good source of revenue for the Semiconductor Products Division (SPD) as Motorola was a long term leader in electronic packaging of semiconductor and power chips. The customer support was very good and much appreciated by the customers and product designers, but the department that did the work was under manufacturing management that was headed up by a man who was skilled politically, did not know how to manage in the best sense, and eventually "gutted" the department to reduce costs. At the same time he purged the semiconductor research area of many skilled scientists especially if they had worked for IBM at one time. He had a very public and unabashed dislike of anyone that had worked for IBM. It was leadership like his that I predicted would lead to the sale of SPD which happened after I left. It is now the most leveraged semiconductor producer in the US and known as Freescale Semiconductor.

The reason Freescale has survived I believe is the innovation of the engineers not the manufacturing people present when I was there.

One product that was ready to announce was a solder bump chip on a plastic BGA and the preliminary reliability tests showed there was insufficient barrier metal in the solder bump area and the solder was forming inter-metallics with the copper lines on the semiconductor and causing an open. I was approached by two high level men working for the manufacturing manager, one of whom I respected very much. The one I thought was in his position just because he was a yes man threatened me to try and get me to say the device was OK to release to customers. The man I respected tried to persuade me to say the device was OK and we could fix it later. My answer was they and their boss could release the part any time they wanted. I was not in a organizational line that had any approval or disapproval responsibility. They were mad and said if I would not "give it my stamp of approval" I was so respected the people that had approval and disapproval responsibility would go by my opinion. They could override all of us but did not. In my view they knew it was wrong and wanted someone else to do their work for them. It was just another example in my long career that once in a while you ran into organizational people with very low ethical standards and depended on their political moves to keep their jobs. In this case the man I had respected had all the tools to be successful on his own, but tied his "coat tails" to a high level manager as his route to success.

Outside of managing a very skilled mix of talent for my time with Motorola I made several disclosures and received an invention award with a couple of additional links to the award and one patent (bump patent) jointly with Stuart Greer another ex-IBMer. One of the presentations I made was in Berlin and it was about BGA reliability put together on the work that our department had done and we made the results available to others in the electronic packaging community. A trip that I was lucky to go on was to go with a vice-president and a director of Motorola to accompany them to Japan to a computer conference and we visited Hitachi on the coast near Tokyo and visited another facility in Nagano just prior to their hosting the Winter Olympics. It was at the Hitachi printed circuit facility in Hitachi City that I saw workers wearing rubber boots while sloshing through shallow chemical laced water on the production line. And this was a leading company in a country that claimed to be so environmentally sensitive!

Somewhere near the end of my time at Motorola I was asked to head up a corporate team to address getting rid of lead in solder as there was a big move to please environmentalists. This was an environmental "cause" at the time and cost the country many millions of dollars. Minimizing lead is an admirable goal and lead can easily be recycled from consumer products by making people turn in old electronics which is done in Europe. In this country we had millions of tons of lead-acid batteries used in cars and industrial equipment with little conscious recycling and it seemed to me that the large problem was mostly ignored and the small problem became the big deal politically. Solders for electronics without lead tend to be brittle and fail readily under a lot of conditions. Today most solders do not use lead but incorporate metals like cadmium, bismuth, and others that cause another set of environmental problems since we don't recycle electronics very well in this country. Most of the time the electronics that are turned in by conscientious consumers get shipped out of the country to poor areas like parts of India and Bangladesh where the very poor remove the materials and components (often re-sold on the international markets as new) at great health risk to themselves so we have not really solved the environmental problem we just shipped to another part of the planet. This does not make me feel good, but environmentalists are generally quiet about this and are not actively seeking true healthy recycling here in this country. Europe has found it to be very beneficial and have found that although gold on connectors and PCBs is only millionths of an inch thick there is more gold per weight on electronics than the best ores in the ground.

References

Authors Patents:
US 6107180 A
Forming a seed layer over the bump pads, then copper, then tin layer using evaporation process covering copper layer, forming lead stand-off structure, depositing eutectic layer of tine-lead solder over bump pads and reflowing the eutectic.

US 3345276 A
Surface treatment for magnesium alloys

NASA Technical Documents:
NASA Technical Memorandum, NASA-™-X-53384, The Astrionics System of Saturn Launch Vehicles, by Rudolph Decher, Astrionics Laboratory, George C. Marshall Space Flight Center, Huntsville, AL

NASA Technical Note NASA TN D-5869, Description and Performance of The Saturn Launch Vehicle's Navigation, Guidance, and Control Sytem, by Walter Haeussermann, George C. Marshall Space Flight Center, Marshall Space Flight Center, AL, 35812 July 1970

Instrument Unit Fact Sheet, Saturn V New Reference, changed December 1968

EE Times, July 20, 2009
Apollo ULD module: flip chip, 45 years ago

TECHSEARCH INTERNATIONAL RESUME 23 Dec, 2014, TechSearch International, Inc. 4801 Spicewood Springs Rd, Austin, TX 78759
Employees: E. Jan Vardaman, president and founder, Dr. Frank J. Bachner, Senior Analyst, Karen Carpenter, Senior Analyst, Charles Cohn, Senior Analyst, Dr. Timothy G. Lenihan, Senior Analyst, Linda C. Mathew, Senior Analyst, and Robert (Bob) Munroe) Senior Analyst.

IBM-FSD Brochure: High Technology Computer Demonstration Product for NASA "HTC Advanced Aerospace Computer" 74-67H-011

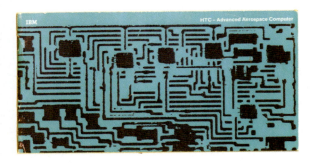

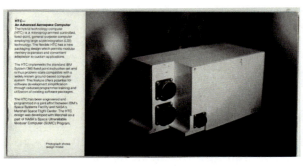

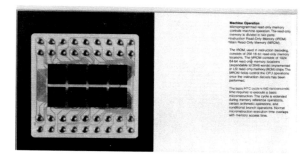

AN ENGINEER'S SPACE RACE STORIES AND MORE

Made in the USA
Middletown, DE
05 July 2021